D1172780

Praise for *Last Words of Jesus*

In *Last Words of Jesus,* Stu Epperson leads us in worship from the foot of the Cross. With thoughtful sensitivity and depth of insight, Stu helps the reader connect the dots between Creation, the Cross, and the Crown as he draws back the veil on the personal meaning and powerful implication behind the words. This book was a blessing to me. I commend it to you.

—Anne Graham Lotz, best-selling author
and president of AnGeL Ministries

Who can doubt that the last words of Jesus on the Cross contain unfathomable treasures of wisdom and power? But how many of us have knowledge that even scratches the surface of those treasures? My dear friend Stu Epperson's *Last Words of Jesus* comes to the rescue! It has profound insights into perhaps the most important event in the history of the world, and it's all told with warmth and passion. Highly recommended!

—Eric Metaxas, *New York Times* best-selling author of *Miracles*
and *Bonhoeffer: Pastor, Martyr, Prophet, Spy*

Stu Epperson is having an incredible impact for the cause of Christ. Through his growing network of Christian radio stations, he is providing believers with solid biblical truth 24/7. He adds to that God-honoring work with his new book, *Last Words of Jesus.* You will be encouraged in God's perfect plan and simultaneously exhorted to take a step of faith in your personal walk with Christ. These are powerful words that every believer should embrace.

—Jonathan Falwell, senior pastor of
Thomas Road Baptist Church, Lynchburg, VA

This is a wonderful "be still and understand just how much I love you" book. *Last Words of Jesus* is a treasure of truth. Beautifully and sensitively written, combining Scripture with touching insights, Stu takes you to the foot of the cross and draws you into God's waiting arms. And there, as you listen carefully to Jesus, you discover how very precious you are to Him . . . even when you were His enemy, even when you sinned. It makes you want to love your Lord even more!

—Kay Arthur, co-founder, Precept Ministries International

I'm grateful for my friend Stu Epperson's careful, thoughtful look at the most important moment in human history. Whether you are a seeker looking into these things for the first time, or a believer in search of deeper insight, you'll find much in here to both challenge and encourage you.

—J. D. Greear, PhD, author of *Jesus, Continued . . . Why the Spirit inside You Is Better Than Jesus beside You* and *Gospel: Recovering the Power That Made Christianity Revolutionary*

The last words of Jesus from the cross are deeply treasured by Christians and for good reason. Our reflection upon those words helps us to understand who Christ is and why He died, and why the gospel is such good news. In this book, Stu Epperson reminds us of the importance of these words and of the spiritual riches contained within these texts. Christians will be greatly blessed by this work.

—R. Albert Mohler Jr., president, Southern Baptist Theological Seminary

Stu Epperson has been on the front lines of spreading the gospel to the masses for years through his work in Christian radio. Now, in his first book, Stu breaks down each of the short but powerful statements Jesus made in His final hours, showing how those words impact us today—and for eternity. This is probably the most powerful sermon Jesus ever gave, but it's the one we often overlook. Don't miss it!

—Dave Ramsey, *New York Times* best-selling author
and nationally syndicated radio show host

The last words of anyone are extremely important. However, the last words of Jesus tower above all others because of who He was. Stu Epperson has given us a well-researched, in-depth account in the *Last Words of Jesus*. If taken seriously, these words will change your life. I highly recommend this book.

—Gary Chapman, PhD, author of *The Five Love Languages*

This wonderfully insightful book is about the greatest of all preachers, as He preached the greatest of all sermons. This was a seven-point sermon that was preached with more than human words. It was a proclamation of love for guilty sinners, heralded from the greatest of all pulpits—the Cross upon which our redemption was purchased.

—Ray Comfort, best-selling author,
cohost of *The Way of the Master*

This book on the sayings of Jesus from the Cross is realistic, direct, and applicable. No matter how often you have meditated on the famous words of Jesus, you will see them in new light through the lens of this young author. Stu eschews platitudes and prefers to confront us directly by describing Jesus' suffering and what following Him should mean for us. Read this book and repent.

—Dr. Erwin W. Lutzer, pastor of The Moody Church, Chicago

Stu Epperson Jr. applies sound biblical interpretation and penetrating contemplation to the final utterances of Christ from the cross. The result is a work of compelling writing by which the Holy Spirit can evoke within each reader deep gratitude and love for their Savior, King Jesus!

—Hank Hanegraaff, president of Christian Research Institute
and host of *Bible Answer Man*

Draw near. See Christ bleeding for you on the cross. And listen carefully. His last words may be His best words. My dear friend Stu Epperson always speaks with passion for Christ. Now, with this compelling prose, he speaks of the passion of Christ. *Last Words of Jesus* searches the depths of Christ's sacrifice on the cross and reveals the depths of God's redeeming love.

—Alan D. Wright, author of *Free Yourself, Be Yourself,*
pastor of Reynolda Church, radio teacher,
and president, Sharing the Light Ministries

Through the *Last Words of Jesus*, you will experience a fresh encounter with the Christ and will come to understand how His powerful words continue to change lives today and for eternity.

—Dr. Tony Evans, senior pastor of Oak Cliff Bible Fellowship,
president of The Urban Alternative

Stu Epperson in his book *Last Words of Jesus* brilliantly helps readers recognize that as they train their eyes upon the crucified Savior, they find Jesus' eyes are really focused upon them.

—Dr. Rob Peters, senior pastor of
Calvary Baptist Church, Winston-Salem, N.C.

Thank you, Stu Epperson, for taking us deeper into the seminal event in history! I pray this book will be therapy for your soul. With so much pain in our world, we need this cogent and refreshing reminder to take our pain to the only One who bore all our pain. And to the only place of true, lasting healing—the glorious cross of Christ.

—Dr. Tim Clinton, president,
American Association of Christian Counselors

Stu Epperson shows us that the words Jesus said on the cross were not the end of the story but the beginning of the gospel. The *Last Words of Jesus* is not about death but about life. How are we to live in light of Jesus' sacrificial death? This book shows us how.

—Gregory Alan Thornbury, PhD,
president of The King's College in New York City

LAST
WORDS
OF JESUS

FIRST STEPS TO
A RICHER LIFE

Stu Epperson, Jr.

WORTHY
Inspired

CONTENTS

To Jules, Hope, Gracie, Joy, and Faith

FOREWORD

BY DAVID JEREMIAH

Several years ago, a friend gave me a book that told the stories behind the last words spoken by famous people before they died. Most of these statements were made by those who knew they were near death. Some were spoken when death came unexpectedly. But in each case, the last words seemed to represent what these men and women embraced, and they revealed either the hope or hopelessness of their lives.

In the New Testament, we are given the opportunity to hear the last words of the two greatest personalities who ever walked upon this earth: Jesus Christ, the Son of God, and His great apostle, Paul.

Paul's last words have been preserved for us in the book of 2 Timothy. The seven last words of Jesus are scattered throughout the four Gospels. While we refer to these sayings as the last words of Jesus, we would be more accurate to say they were our Lord's last words before His crucifixion and death. They were not really His last words, since He said many other important things between His resurrection and ascension.

Sermons and books on the seven last words of Jesus have been continuously produced over the years from one generation to another. So why should we be interested in another book about this subject?

I have known Stuart Epperson for over twenty years, and he approaches the writing of a book with the same genuineness and enthusiasm with which he approaches life. That is what makes this book unique. The author wants us to see the powerful practicality of the legacy Jesus left to us with His final sayings.

His treatment of these sacred sayings is theologically correct and contextually accurate. But with his many quotes, stories, and poems, he also helps us look into the heart of our Lord as He suffers His final moments on the cross.

You will especially enjoy the stories that Stuart tells from the many people who have called into his daily radio talk show. Their questions are real, and they illustrate why this book is so needed!

Beginning with a word of forgiveness for those who have betrayed Him, Jesus turns to the repentant thief, who is hanging on a cross beside Him, and offers a word of hope and salvation. Looking down and seeing His mother, He expresses His love. Looking up, He cries out to the Father in the anguish of abandonment. From His suffering body comes the cry of thirst, and to the whole world He cries, "It is finished!" With His final breath He commends His spirit to the Father in heaven.

As he tells the story of Jesus' first word of forgiveness, Stuart Epperson asks if we have those we need to forgive.

At the end of the chapter on the repentant thief, we are asked on which side of the cross we find ourselves. Have we refused our Lord's salvation or have we repented?

As the author tells the story of our Lord's love for His mother, we cannot help but hear the piercing voice of the Holy Spirit confronting us with our responsibility to honor our parents and love our families.

Hearing the anguish of our Lord's "Why hast thou forsaken me?" we are made to see the awful price that was paid for our redemption. The Father was separated from the Son for three long hours. The most intimate relationship suffered the most horrible separation.

The pain of the suffering Savior is heard in the words, "I thirst." And we are challenged to remember that Jesus suffered that thirst so that He might be able to say, "He who believes in me shall never thirst."

When He cried, "It is finished," our Lord announced

that what He had come to do was accomplished . . . never to be needed again. Stuart Epperson brings these words of Jesus right into our daily lives. Because "it is finished," we can get off the treadmill of performance for God. It is no longer about what we do for God; it is about what God has done for us! Settle down into that truth and see if that doesn't remove some stress.

Having come from the Father, Jesus returned to the Father with His final words of "into thy hands I commend my spirit." And we are likewise called to submit ourselves into the hands of the Father.

As I always do, I read this book with a pen in hand. I underlined something on every page, and I recommend you do the same. You will read so many things that you will not want to forget.

I am honored to provide this foreword to my friend's first book, and I recommend it to you with all of my heart.

He was oppressed, and he was afflicted,
yet he opened not his mouth: he is brought as
a lamb to the slaughter, and as a sheep before
her shearers is dumb, so he openeth not his mouth.

—

Isaiah 53:7 KJV

SEVEN WORDS OF LIFE FROM THE TREE OF DEATH

The stage was set. The night was dark. The forces of evil, visible and invisible, viciously swarmed upon one Man. Not just any man, but the One who carried the weight of the world on His back. He is the only Man who, with just one word, could have instantly eradicated all His foes—for He was the One Person who had the Word of God flowing through Him. In fact, He was the very Word of God (John 1:1).

But He opened not his mouth. Not a single sermon was spoken by the greatest Teacher of all time—who had taught for three years in synagogues, on boats, atop mountains, and across the Galilean countryside. Not so much as a single mutter, syllable, or utterance came from the One who always knew just what to say and how to say it perfectly. There was nothing but deafening silence from the One who only had to speak and the blind saw, the lame leapt, the lepers were healed, and the dead were raised.

Jesus spoke not a word in His own defense to the chief priests, the Sanhedrin, Herod, Pilate, the mob, or the soldiers.

- He "kept silent" (Matthew 26:63).
- He "answered him not one word" (Matthew 27:14).
- He "answered nothing" (Mark 15:3).
- He "still answered nothing" (Mark 15:5).
- He "answered him nothing" (Luke 23:9).
- He "gave him no answer" (John 19:9).
- "When He was reviled, did not revile in return: when He suffered, he did not threaten" (1 Peter 2:23).

He who spoke the universe into existence stood silent in the face of heinous slander and abuse. He quietly endured the shame of a jeering crowd. Barely a word throughout the betrayal . . . the interrogation . . . the trial . . . the questions . . . the scourging . . . the torture . . . the mocking . . . the insults.

Profound silence emanated from the One who bore infinite duress. His deafening silence remained unbroken all the way to the Place of the Skull.

And He, bearing His cross, went out to a place called the Place of a Skull, which is called in Hebrew, Golgotha. (John 19:17)

And then . . . Jesus opened His mouth:

> Seven Words of Life He cried,
> Seven Words with His last breath.
> Seven Words as Jesus died,
> Seven Words of Life from the Tree of Death.[1]

What were these "Seven Words" from the Cross, and why are they significant?

It is striking that Jesus uttered from the Cross *seven* sayings. Seven is the number that Scripture regards as "sacred and complete."[2]

> *O kingly silence of our Lord!*
> *O wordless wonder of the Word!*
> *O hush, that while all Heaven is awed,*
> *Makes music in the ear of God!*
> *Silence—yet with a sevenfold stroke*
> *Seven times a wondrous bell there broke*
> *Upon the cross, when Jesus spoke.*[3]

Listen as the greatest Preacher of all time gives seven of the greatest sermons in history.

Seven messages delivered from His wooden pulpit—a rough-hewn Roman cross.

Seven earth-shattering statements proclaimed on an outdoor stage morbidly shaped like a skull.

The seven Last Words of Jesus.

Then said Jesus, Father, forgive them;
for they know not what they do.

Luke 23:34 KJV

FATHER, FORGIVE THEM; FOR THEY KNOW NOT WHAT THEY DO

A WORD OF PRAYER

A little more than two thousand years ago, Jesus Christ hung on a cross on a busy road just outside Jerusalem at a place called Golgotha. Victims of crucifixion endured horrific torture resulting in agonizing death. This punishment was reserved for the worst of criminals. With a relentless Middle Eastern sun beating down, we find Jesus mounted between two thieves.

The scene at the place known as the Place of the Skull was solemn and sorrowful as Jesus, innocent of all wrongdoing, was nailed to His cross. Dramatically contrasting with the weeping mourners were the raucous and mocking

Roman soldiers, casting lots for a chance to win Jesus' garment as He hung dying. Just hours earlier Jesus had stood stained and bloodied before Pontius Pilate. A riotous mob stirred by the religious leaders had clamored for Jesus' death when given the chance to free Him.

Opening Prayer

Remarkably, the last words of Jesus start with prayer. After all the torture, flogging, abuse, and grueling journey to Calvary, Christ prays. In history's darkest moment He finds Himself in prayer's familiar light. Imagine the audacity of someone saying, "Let's begin this human sacrifice of the Son of God with a word of prayer!"

At least eight of Jesus' prayers are recorded in Scripture, but this one is unique. He will pray as the Lamb being led to the slaughter, the Mediator interceding for sinners, and the High Priest atoning for sins. Consider the profundity of this most incredible moment.[1]

The implication of Jesus' praying during His last hours on the Cross is profound. In the words of Arthur W. Pink:

The first of the seven cross sayings of our Lord presents him in the attitude of prayer. How significant! How instructive! His public ministry had opened with prayer (Luke 3:21), and here we see it closing in prayer. Surely he is an example! No longer might those hands minister to the sick, for they are nailed to the cross; no longer may those feet carry him on errands of mercy, for they are fastened to the cruel tree; no longer may Jesus engage in instructing the Apostles, for they have forsaken him and fled—how does he occupy himself? In the ministry of prayer! What a lesson for us.[2]

Jesus is praying for His tormentors and dying for them at the same time! The prophet Isaiah says it this way: "He bore the sin of many, and made intercession for the transgressors" (Isaiah 53:12).

Hanging on a Tree of Death in open shame
Nails pierce His hands and feet,
He quietly bears our blame.
Bleeding and battered, a covering for
the nakedness of Adam's sin
Behold the lamb dying, with no voice saying
"spare the Son"
Yet as blood flows from His wounds
Life flows from His words.[3]

Prayer marked the beginning of Jesus' ministry (Mark 1:35) and prayer consumed His life and practice (Matthew 6:9–13; Luke 6:12). The night before Jesus uttered His famous last words, He had prayed in the Garden of Gethsemane (Matthew 26:36).

And here at the Cross, Jesus prayed to His . . .

"Father"

Jesus prayed to the One with whom He shared deep intimate fellowship from all eternity. The One who led Him, fed Him, walked with Him, and loved Him. The One He called Father throughout the four Gospels. The One whose business He always attended (Luke 2:49). The One who could easily step in and mightily defend His only Son.

Instead, Jesus calls upon His Father to . . .

"Forgive"

Forgive them? Are you serious? Why not destroy them for killing an innocent man—and for executing the God-man!

Savor the words of forgiveness spoken by the Teacher from Galilee who now practices what He preached, as recorded in Matthew:

- Blessed are you when people insult you and persecute you (5:11).

- Bless those who curse you (5:44).
- Forgive your debtors (6:12).
- If you forgive others, your heavenly Father will also forgive you (6:14).
- Forgive until seventy times seven times (18:21–22).

How amazing! The only One on earth who needs no forgiveness is petitioning His Father to forgive. Hear this Word of Life from the lips of a dying Savior. See Him dying to purchase life and forgiveness for undeserving people like you and me.

The Father can be called upon to forgive because "He who did not spare His own Son, but delivered Him up for us all, how shall He not with Him also freely give us all things?" (Romans 8:32).

Seventeenth-century German biographer and pastor F. W. Krummacher marveled at the glory of Christ as He forgave His tormentors: "'Forgive them!' What? What does He mean? Surely not the servants of Satan who have nailed Him to the cross—the heartless brutes. . . . Christ was admirable in His transfiguration on Mount Tabor; but here He shines in superior light."[4]

No others who have claimed deity offer such a magnanimous prayer on behalf of their tormentors. The only way to live is through the only God who forgives.

As blood flows from His wounds, forgiveness flows from His words.

These words of forgiveness are prayed for . . .

"Them"

Jesus petitions the Father to forgive "them." But who are *they*?

- The Roman soldiers?
- The religious leaders?
- The deserting disciples?
- The apathetic bystanders?
- The malicious mob?
- The entire fallen race of Adam—past, present, and future?
- The three thousand who would be forgiven at Pentecost?
- Or perhaps He was praying for *you*!

Prayer was the last thing on the minds of those at the scene of the Cross. However, prayer was the first thing that came out of the mouth of the One they placed on the Cross.

Fallen creatures rarely see their need for prayer, because of what Jesus says next:

"Father, forgive them . . .

"For They Know Not What They Do"

Picture yourself standing at the Cross participating in this bloody spectacle. Have we any idea what our sin did to the Savior? If those at the scene didn't know, then how much more clueless are we centuries removed from the event?

Yet now, brethren, I know that you did it in ignorance,
as did also your rulers. (Acts 3:17)

Had they known [the wisdom of God], they would not
have crucified the Lord of glory. (1 Corinthians 2:8)

Remarkably, the deeper the blows of sin ravage the Innocent One, the wider His healing forgiveness flows forth. Perhaps King David knew what his sin did to Jesus. In Psalm 51:4, David writes, "Against You, You only, have I sinned, and done this evil in Your sight."

For centuries, people have debated the question "Who killed Jesus?" At whose feet do we lay the blame? Was it Pilate? The Jewish leaders? The traitorous Judas? The ruthless Roman soldiers? This is the question of the ages—and a question that could change your life.

A. W. Tozer says it was all of the above, *and* you and me. Those on Golgotha that day were guilty, but we are too. Our anger, dishonesty, hatred, jealousy, carnality—all our fleshly sins—joined with their sins in putting Jesus on the Cross. "We may as well admit it," Tozer concludes. "Every one of us in Adam's race had a share in putting Him on the cross!"[5]

Seventeenth-century Scottish poet Horatius Bonar captured this inescapable truth in his haunting hymn:

> *I see the crowd in Pilate's hall,*
> *Their furious cries I hear;*
> *Their shouts of "Crucify!" appall,*
> *Their curses fill mine ear.*
> *And of that shouting multitude*
> *I feel that I am one;*
> *And in the din of voices rude,*
> *I recognize my own. . . .*
>
> *Around the Cross the throng I see,*
> *That mock the Sufferer's groan,*
> *Yet still my voice it seems to be,*
> *As if I mocked alone.*
>
> *'Twas I that shed the sacred Blood;*
> *I nailed him to the tree;*
> *I crucified the Christ of God;*
> *I joined the mockery.*[6]

Stop for a moment and ponder your sin and guilt that nailed Jesus to the tree. Think about your own deep need for His forgiveness. Have you called out for the forgiving grace of the gospel?

Picture your worst enemy, someone who has wronged or wounded you deeply. Are you ready to take your pain to the Cross and pray with Christ, "Father, forgive them"?

Charles Spurgeon, the eighteenth-century preacher, urges us to keep "looking into those five wounds, and studying that marred face, and counting every purple drop that flowed from His hands and feet, and side. . . . Smite your breast because you see in Christ your sin."[7]

Have you been forgiven?

And you, being dead in your trespasses and the uncircumcision of your flesh, He has made alive together with him, having forgiven you all trespasses. (Colossians 2:13)

Have you experienced these last words of Jesus by forgiving those who have wronged you?

Be kind one to another, tenderhearted, forgiving one another, even as God in Christ forgave you. (Ephesians 4:32)

The Supernatural Power of Forgiveness

Could you forgive someone who murdered your family?

I once opened my national radio talk show with this question, and as you can imagine, the phone lines immediately lit up. My guest that day was Laura Waters Hinson. This deeply vexing issue confronted multitudes of Rwandans in the aftermath of their country's massive, bloody, and genocidal civil war of 1994. Moms and dads, sisters and brothers, and grandmas and grandpas were brutally murdered by rival tribes—and not by the quick shot of a gun, but by the savage thrusts of axes, machetes, and farming tools.

In her riveting documentary *As We Forgive*, Hinson chronicles the supernatural power of forgiveness that healed the Rwandan nation. A Christ-centered forgiveness penetrated this place where there weren't enough prisons to house all the guilty.[8]

Or consider the remarkable testimony of forgiveness as told by Steve Saint. Four decades ago, Steve's father, Nate Saint—along with four other missionaries—was speared to death while bringing the gospel to the Auca Indians in South America. Despite his father's brutal murder at the hands of this savage tribe, Steve's family chose to extend them forgiveness. "Today," Steve says, "I have a home among these people . . . and some of the very men who speared my father have become substitute grandfathers to my children."[9]

Warning: Unforgiveness Is Hazardous to Your Health

There's a growing wealth of scientific support for the popular adage, "Unforgiveness is like pouring a cup of poison for your enemy and then drinking it yourself." Modern medicine has uncovered some remarkable yet not surprising data linking unforgiveness directly to a person's physical health. Unforgiveness causes a host of stress and anxiety-related health problems, while forgiveness reduces your health risk and "can actually strengthen your immune system."[10]

The world-renowned Mayo Clinic has correlated acts of forgiveness with positive, healthy outcomes. Their studies show that letting go of bitterness leads to lower blood pressure, fewer stress-related illnesses, healthier relationships, and reduced risk of alcohol or drug abuse.[11]

In contrast, the Bible sends a dire warning that withholding forgiveness will absolutely destroy you:

> *Look carefully lest anyone fall short of the grace of God; lest any root of bitterness springing up cause trouble, and by this many become defiled.* (Hebrews 12:15)

A Mighty Current of Forgiveness

This first Word of Life from the Tree of Death sets in motion a mighty current of forgiveness that transcends centuries and redeems thousands. Jesus' words can heal the deepest wounds—even wounds inflicted by someone who murdered your family.

Have these words healed you? Have you found in Christ the payment for your sin? As Charles Spurgeon urges, "Let us go to Calvary to learn how we may be forgiven; and then let us linger there to learn how we may forgive. There shall we see what sin is, as it murders the Lord of love."[12]

Here at the bloody scene, these forgiving Words of Life spoken from the Tree of Death could have been Christ's prayer for His *neighbor*. Another man was hanging in similar form just a few feet away . . . a certain thief.

SCRIPTURAL REFLECTIONS
ON THE LAST WORDS OF JESUS

Father, Forgive Them;
for They Know Not What They Do

1. "Blessed is he whose transgression is forgiven, whose sin is covered" (Psalm 32:1).

2. "Against You, You only, have I sinned, and done this evil in Your sight—that You might be found just when You speak, and blameless when You judge" (Psalm 51:4).

3. "In return for my love they are my accusers, but I give myself to prayer" (Psalm 109:4).

4. "If You, LORD, should mark iniquities, O Lord, who could stand? But there is forgiveness with You, that You may be feared" (Psalm 130:3–4).

5. "'Come now, and let us reason together,' says the LORD, 'though your sins are like scarlet, they shall be as white as snow; though they are red like crimson, they shall be as wool'" (Isaiah 1:18).

6. "He shall see the labor of His soul, and be satisfied. By His knowledge My righteous Servant shall justify many, for He shall bear their iniquities" (Isaiah 53:11).

7. "To the Lord our God belong mercy and forgiveness, though we have rebelled against Him" (Daniel 9:9).

8. "Blessed are the merciful, for they shall obtain mercy" (Matthew 5:7).

9. "But I say to you who hear: Love your enemies, do good to those who hate you, bless those who curse you, and pray for those who spitefully use you" (Luke 6:27–28).

10. "Then he knelt down and cried out with a loud voice, 'Lord, do not charge them with this sin.' And when he had said this, he fell asleep" (Acts 7:60).

11. "Bless those who persecute you; bless and do not curse" (Romans 12:14).

12. "In Him we have redemption through His blood, the forgiveness of sins, according to the riches of His grace" (Ephesians 1:7).

13. "And be kind to one another, tenderhearted, forgiving one another, even as God in Christ forgave you" (Ephesians 4:32).

14. "In whom we have redemption through his blood, even the forgiveness of sins" (Colossians 1:14 KJV).

15. "And you, being dead in your trespasses and the uncircumcision of your flesh, He has made alive together with Him, having forgiven you all trespasses" (Colossians 2:13).

16. "For to this you were called; because Christ also suffered for us, leaving us an example, that you should follow His steps: 'Who committed no sin, nor was deceit found in his mouth'; who, when He was reviled, did not revile in return; when He suffered, He did not threaten, but committed Himself to Him who judges righteously" (1 Peter 2:21–23).

17. "Not returning evil for evil or reviling for reviling, but on the contrary blessing, knowing that you were called to this, that you may inherit a blessing" (1 Peter 3:9).

18. "And from Jesus Christ, the faithful witness, the firstborn from the dead, and the ruler over the kings of the earth. To Him who loved us and washed us from our sins in His own blood" (Revelation 1:5).

LAST WORDS, FIRST STEPS

Chapter 1 Discussion Questions

1. Why does Jesus begin His last recorded words from the Cross with a word of prayer?

2. What does it mean to truly forgive and be forgiven?

3. Who was Jesus praying for?

4. What role did your sin play in the crucifixion of Jesus?

5. Is it more difficult to forgive or to seek forgiveness? Why?

6. What are some of the consequences of unforgiveness—both present and eternal?

7. What are the first steps to being eternally forgiven?

Verily I say unto thee,
today shalt thou be with me in paradise.

—

Luke 23:43 KJV

TODAY SHALT THOU
BE WITH ME IN PARADISE

WORD OF PARDON

The man who baptized Jeffrey Dahmer was one of the more fascinating guests on my syndicated radio talk show, *Truth Talk Live*. Dahmer was a sadistic serial killer who infamously ate his victims. Found guilty and sentenced to death, he turned to God before his death.

What was supposed to be a cordial, inspirational exchange instead turned into a spirited debate. At the heart of the discussion were such issues as: Was it baptism or believing in Jesus that saved Dahmer? How legitimate are death-row conversions? Can someone as evil as Jeffrey Dahmer be redeemed by Christ's grace?

The answers to these hard questions can be found as you and I approach Calvary. Life and death and heaven and hell are directly encountered in this famous narrative of the thief on the Cross—the second of Jesus Christ's Words of Life from the Tree of Death.

Two Thieves, Two Prayers

Have you ever wondered why so many churches display three wooden crosses on their grounds instead of just one? The redemptive power of Jesus Christ is traced back to His Cross, and His alone. So why are three crosses often showcased? Is there a message here?

Perhaps three crosses represent the state of all men: the *unredeemed,* the *redeemed,* and the *Redeemer.* Perhaps we're all guilty as thieves and find our place on one side of the Cross or the other. Just as there are two sides to every story, in this story there are two eternally different results.

How many people called out for salvation at the scene of the Cross? The answer may surprise you: *two* (not counting the centurion's remarkable confession in Luke 23:47). *Two* sinners' prayers were offered that day from the *two* crosses on either side of the Savior.

In this account we have *two* robbers, *two* requests, *two* responses, and *two* results. The first demanded, "If You are the Christ, save Yourself and us" (Luke 23:39). The second implored, "Lord, remember me when You come into Your kingdom" (Luke 23:42).

Bible commentator Warren Wiersbe notes, "It was providential that Jesus was crucified *between* the two thieves, for this gave them both equal access to the Savior. Both could read Pilate's superscription, 'This Is Jesus of Nazareth, the King of the Jews,' and both could watch Him as He graciously gave His life for the sins of the world."[1]

"Save Yourself"

The request "Save Yourself," made by the first thief, was impossible to grant. How could Christ save that wretched man if He first saved Himself from impending death? Hadn't this method of salvation and deliverance been prophesied concerning the One who would come as the Messiah and Redeemer? In blurting out those challenging words, the thief's shrill voice joined the scorning chorus of the mob and soldiers who were goading Jesus to demonstrate His power to save Himself—to prove to them that He truly was the Son of God.

They didn't realize that Jesus is the only One who could save anyone! If Jesus had acted upon their demands and come down from the Cross, He would have, in effect, damned the recalcitrant thief and everyone else to eternal hell.

Had our Savior heeded these confronting calls, what

kind of Savior would He be? Who else but the Son of God could atone for that man's sin? The first thief blindly asked for double death. Had Christ granted his request to come down from the cross, the thief may have *lived* for a while past the cross—but would have ultimately still *died* in his sins. The first Adam took this option, and as a consequence our entire race has pursued death ever since. We cry out, "Save yourself!" or protest, "This isn't the best way," and demand, "Fix my circumstances and put me back in control"—all in self-serving shortsightedness.

"Save Yourself! Come down from the Cross!"

Was this the first time Jesus heard this appeal? Not at all. Throughout Christ's ministry, others had uttered similar words:

- Satan, in the wilderness (Matthew 4:1–10; Mark 1:13; Luke 4:1–13)
- Peter, under Satan's influence (Matthew 16:22)
- The mob (Matthew 27:40; Mark 15:30)
- The chief priests, the scribes, and elders (Matthew 27:41–42; Mark 15:31)
- Both thieves initially (Matthew 27:43-44; Mark 15:32)

- The people, the rulers, and the soldiers (Luke 23:35–37)

The first thief prays for just enough of Christ to keep comfortable and stay at ease. His Jesus is a palatable, un-bloodied, and dignified version of Christ, minus His barbaric death. Like the thief, our human nature seeks everything about Christ—except the raw and agonizing truth of the shameful Cross.

Seek a Christ without His Cross and you'll get sweet-sounding philosophies, tragically leading to eternal hell. The first thief, even in his final breaths, calls out for a self-serving kind of salvation that seeks a reprieve from certain judgment and deserving punishment. It is at best a sickening sweet balm reeking only of a deceptive pragmatism that will work for us. But *this* type of human salvation will never save the thief or transform anyone. Like the thousands who flocked to Jesus in John 6, thief number one wanted a nice meal of miracle bread, not the broken bread of death.

The first thief also says . . .

"Save Us!"

The first blasphemous request renders the second pointless. Nonetheless, it is profound to note that these are some of the earliest sinner's prayers pleading for salvation, and they occurred at the Cross. How sad that this man on death row didn't recognize that the answer to his greatest need—a Savior—was just a few feet away. How many skeptics have boasted, "If I could have been there and seen Him dying, I would have believed!" This first thief saw the Savior dying, saw Him impart the message of forgiveness to the crowd and pardon his comrade; but shockingly, he rejects the gift of salvation.

The first thief wanted collective salvation for himself and his fellow offender, demonstrated by his self-centered prayer: "Save us!"

Why was this seemingly unselfish request so damnable? Like so many, he didn't see his personal, desperate need for the blood of Jesus to be shed for him. The thief was worrying about *we* and *us* and not worrying about his own soul on the Day of Judgment. Like an old country preacher once said, "God doesn't have any grandchildren!" Tragically, thief number one was only moments away from a judgment supremely more severe than that of a Roman cross—a judgment hastened by his outright rejection of the Man in the Middle. He was so close, yet so far away.

There's no other way than the way of the Cross. Without the Tree of Death, there could be no Words of Life!

How did Christ respond to this man's plea? Only with chilling silence.

The thief on the other side replied with a righteous rebuke: "Do you not even fear God, seeing you are under the same condemnation?" (Luke 23:40).

Let's examine the second thief's famous prayer, which starts with . . .

"Lord"

This revolting, reprobate robber is the only person at the ghastly scene to openly confess Jesus as "Lord." From his own tree of death he pleads for life. The apostle Paul may have had this thief in mind when he penned the words, "If you confess with your mouth the Lord Jesus" (Romans 10:9).

While the second thief's broken body was suspended *high* in the air, his broken heart was bowed *low* before the Lord of glory. Witness the deathbed conversion of the thief at this moment. Yet, as Matthew Henry observes, "This gives no encouragement to any to put off their repentance, for, though it is certain that true repentance is never too late, it is as certain that late repentance is seldom true."[2]

He continues . . .

"Remember Me"

Jesus last used the word *remember* just hours before in the Upper Room. He said, "Remember me" when speaking of His body and blood as He lifted the bread and wine.

Prophetically, "Remember me" were the words of Joseph to the royal cupbearer, ultimately leading to the salvation of his people (Genesis 40:14, 23; 41:12–13).[3] These powerful words are still invoked centuries later as believers celebrate the sacrament of the Lord's Supper.

These are the same words the second thief uses in his final moments as he witnesses the Passover bread literally being broken and the wine spilled in front of him. Perhaps it's this broken thief who first partakes of the feast of salvation invoking the same word: "remember." Yes, the word *remember* can seem meaningless or downplayed, unless it has to do with life and death. Thief number two was prepared to take the bread, the wine, and the "fellowship of His sufferings" (Philippians 3:10).

The second thief's simple request as a response of faith brushes aside all our modern "sinner's prayer" rules. So humbled in his rigid state, yet so in awe of the majestic King hanging beside him, this dying thief calls out in simple faith, "Remember me." Most likely he was physically closer to Jesus than any other at that place, except for the defiant thief on the other side. This makes one wonder: how could one be so close to the Savior of the world and *not* be saved—especially in such a desperate, fatal position?

Yet only the accused thief gets it, and only he calls out to be *remembered*. This thief recognized that while the three men on Calvary shared a common punishment, there was one thing they did not have in common: the thieves were sinners dying for their own sins, while the Man in the Middle was the Sinless One dying for the sins of others.[4]

What a stark contrast between this thief and his partner in crime! In the same spirit as "I am no longer worthy to be called your son. Make me like one of your hired servants" (Luke 15:19) or "Be merciful to me a sinner" (Luke 18:13), this forlorn thief cries as one "broken" (Psalm 34:18) and "poor in spirit" (Matthew 5:3).

Ask for Christ's mercy and grace from the Cross, and you will experience heaven!

Keep your gaze on the Son of Man, nailed to the Tree that is firmly planted in the middle. On one side hangs an unrepentant and mocking thief who is soon to experience God's wrath. On the other side, in stark contrast, hangs a repentant and humble thief who is soon to experience God's unmerited pardon as he fixes his eyes on his Redeemer.

Across the corridors of redemptive history, whose prayer does God answer?

- The prayer of the Pharisee or the publican?
- The cry of the prodigal or of the older brother?
- The petition of the proud or of the penitent?
- The offering of Cain or the sacrifice of Abel?

Two brothers a sacrifice made;
One brought a lamb,
The other his effort—the toil of his spade.
The younger killed the lamb and was accepted by Another;
The older murdered his brother and was marked
by death like no other.

Two men went to the temple to pray;
The righteous stood proud, disgusted by
the sinner at his side,
The other lowly bowed with barely a word to say;
No salvation to the haughty man, but the sinner
joyously was saved.

Two brothers sought the father's heart to please;
One praised himself—his own righteous condition.
The other begged for mercy with a heart of contrition;
No peace for the elder son
But the younger found salvation.

Two criminals ascended to Calvary, condemned to die;
One joined the hateful throng,
The other listened humbly—his heart to
the middle man drew nigh.
A greater death met the first thief's wrong,

While life everlasting came to the second
from on high.

One man, poor in spirit;
Another, high and pious.
One man, low and humble;
Another, proud and pompous.
Which man are you?[5]

Nothing but silence answers the first thief's arrogant request for salvation.

A completely different answer awaits the second thief. Observe the simplest, most effective sinner's prayer ever prayed: "Lord, remember me."

What led to this moment? The penitent thief sees the rough-hewn shingle labeled "King" hanging above this mysterious Man in the Middle. He hears Him forgive His haters and tormentors. So at the end of his rope he cries out, "Lord, remember me."

Before a person can be saved, he must realize his own sin and weakness. What could the dying thief do? Arthur W. Pink explains, "He could not walk in the paths of righteousness, for there was a nail through either foot. He could not perform any good works, for there was a nail through either hand. He could not turn over a new leaf and live a better life, for he was dying."[6] He could do nothing to be saved, except confess his belief and plead with Jesus to remember him.

This second thief further implores the King of kings: "Remember me . . .

"When Thou Comest into Thy Kingdom"

The fact that the second thief says *when* and not *if* speaks volumes about the depth of this new convert's faith. With heaven and hell set before him, the repentant robber asks for heaven.

Not only does he plead for salvation, but now he also looks forward to the reality to come. With deep hope this thief echoes the voice of Job, who under his own cross of suffering exclaimed, "I know that my Redeemer lives" (Job 19:25). Not only did he know the fellowship of His sufferings, but also the "power of His resurrection" (Philippians 3:10), believing in his heart that God would raise Jesus from the dead (Romans 10:9).

Both criminals ascended the Place of the Skull to die. Both thieves heard the Word of Prayer and Forgiveness from the Man in the Middle. But only *one* would receive a personal word of pardon and be changed forever!

A prayer was answered, a divine pardon was granted, and a price was paid that even the thief's terrible cross could not satisfy.

Hanging on his own tree of death, the thief hears glorious words of life that start with, "Verily, I say unto you . . ."

"Today"

An instant declaration of pardon. No frills, no gimmicks, just unfiltered words of eternal salvation spoken from just a few feet away. *Wham!* A direct hit. No conditions, no exceptions, no prescriptions, no preexisting blemishes, no waiting period.

It's as though the apostle Paul is pleading with this thief: "Behold, now is the accepted time; behold, now is the day of salvation" (2 Corinthians 6:2).

And this salvation is being given to the least likely of candidates . . .

"You"

In this seminal moment in history, to whom does the Messiah demonstrate His mercy? Of all the pedigrees and potential of society's elite who were present at Christ's execution, He addresses the least qualified and lowliest of status, indeed.

Greg Laurie explains, "The Romans reserved crucifixion for the worst, most hardened criminals. We know these men as thieves, but they were likely terrorists, even murderers."[7]

How can this be? Now Jesus has angered His religious tormentors even more! Surely He can do better than this. Why save a thief? Why not a celebrity? Even in this pinnacle moment of redemption, once again the Friend of Sinners stoops down to rescue the sick and not the healthy. He saves the sinner and not the righteous, the poor in spirit and not the haughty.

Perhaps it's to demonstrate our own true condition before Christ. Haven't we all lived like thieves, robbing God, turning from His glory?

Haven't we betrayed the divine imbuement of His own image that He placed on His children in the very beginning?

Haven't we discarded His greater glory and pleasure for our earthly and sinful pleasures? Like this thief, we deserve God's wrath.

But in an instant, a common, worthless, condemned thief becomes a royal son of the Most High and is given a promise of eternal paradise. How can this be? Because another Son hangs next to him, the only One who can take his place and bear his penalty at the same time. This cast-out son of Adam cries out for *redemption* and hears the second Adam, the very Son of God, grant it! He is condemned by man yet justified by God on the same day.

While the first Word of Life proclaimed to the many was more of a shotgun prayer of forgiveness, the second Word of Life spoken to the repentant thief no doubt hit its mark like a rifle's bullet.

The dying thief rejoiced to see
That fountain in his day,
And there may I, though vile as he,
Wash all my sins away.[8]

In an ineffable display of unconditional love, the second thief *dies* with Christ and yet *lives* with Christ (Philippians 1:21). He is instantly and eternally bound to the fate of the Son of Man, who is standing in the middle.

Marvel at how the forgiven thief is miraculously transported from his desperate fate of peril and perishing to a new, blessed state of pardon and peace.

Jesus continues, "Today, you . . .

"Will Be with Me in Paradise"

The second thief finds himself in the *worst* condemned state and the *best* redeemed state simultaneously. Only this intensely personal encounter with Jesus Christ saves him from his imminent encounter with eternal damnation. Who better to identify with Paul's thought in Galatians 2:20: "I have been crucified with Christ"? He was the only one in history who lived that verse—literally!

Also, it's no secret that "with Me" (Luke 23:43) means Jesus *is* the "paradise." While in the garden the night before,

He prayed, "And this is eternal life, that they may know You" (John 17:3). This is a simple yet profound statement of the ultimate glory of knowing Christ.

To know Jesus is to know peace. A man who terrorized and stole for a living, now dying for his evil, is suddenly *reborn* and *transformed*. That transformation has everything to do with his relationship with the Middle Man, his Redeemer.

And if I go and prepare a place for you, I will come again and receive you to Myself; that where I am, there you may be also. (John 14:3)

Pardon granted. Paradise bound. A dead man is reborn!

David Jeremiah explains, "Heaven is where Jesus is. The Bible has many references to his presence there, and when we read it or hear it, the Bible leaves no question about the matter. When we go to heaven, we are going to be with Jesus. Heaven's not about a place; it's about a person!"[9]

The King will enter this kingdom shortly—but not alone. This dramatic scene decisively solves a lot of issues, such as:

- What is the "sinner's prayer"?
- Is it ever too late to be saved?
- Does God ever give up on us?
- How much must one do to earn eternal life?

So many doctrinal issues are solved in this profound exchange. Any notion of good works as being necessary for salvation is refuted by the second thief's immediate welcome into paradise. Here the teachings of purgatory, soul-sleep, and universalism are all disproved as the thief is assured he will be with Jesus in paradise—"today."[10]

Charles Spurgeon states, "The man who was our Lord's last companion on earth was his first companion at the gates of paradise."[11]

Take a moment and ask yourself two important questions:

1. On which side of the Cross are you?
2. Which thief's prayer reflects the state and cry of your heart?

Only one way leads to life, peace, and heaven (John 14:6).

While this Word of Life from the Tree of Death extends an unconditional pardon and paradise for a dying soul, Jesus' next Word will show deep care for the living.

SCRIPTURAL REFLECTIONS
ON THE LAST WORDS OF JESUS

Today Shalt Thou Be with Me in Paradise

1. "The LORD is near to those who have a broken heart, and saves such as have a contrite spirit" (Psalm 34:18).

2. "For as the heavens are high above the earth, so great is His mercy toward those who fear Him. As far as the east is from the west, so far has He removed our transgressions from us" (Psalm 103:11–12).

3. The fruit of the righteous is a tree of life; and he who wins souls is wise" (Proverbs 11:30).

4. "He poured out His soul unto death, and He was numbered with the transgressors, and He bore the sin of many, and made intercession for the transgressors" (Isaiah 53:12).

5. "For thus says the High and Lofty One who inhabits eternity, whose name is Holy; 'I dwell in the high and holy place, with him who has a contrite and humble

spirit, to revive the spirit of the humble, and to revive the heart of the contrite ones'" (Isaiah 57:15).

6. "But go and learn what this means: 'I desire mercy and not sacrifice.' For I did not come to call the righteous, but sinners, to repentance" (Matthew 9:13).

7. "Then two robbers were crucified with Him, one on the right and another on the left" (Matthew 27:38).

8. "With Him they also crucified two robbers, one on His right and the other on His left. So the Scripture was fulfilled which says, 'And He was numbered with the transgressors'" (Mark 15:27–28).

9. "There were also two others, criminals, led with Him to be put to death. And when they had come to the place called Calvary, there they crucified Him, and the criminals, one on the right hand and the other on the left" (Luke 23:32–33).

10. "They crucified Him, and two others with Him, one on either side, and Jesus in the center" (John 19:18).

11. "Now hope does not disappoint, because the love of God has been poured out in our hearts by the Holy Spirit who was given to us. For when we were still without strength, in due time Christ died for the ungodly" (Romans 5:5–6).

12. "If you confess with your mouth the Lord Jesus and believe in your heart that God has raised Him from the dead, you will be saved. For with the heart one believes unto righteousness, and with the mouth confession is made unto salvation" (Romans 10:9–10).

13. "For God did not appoint us to wrath, but to obtain salvation through our Lord Jesus Christ, who died for us, that whether we wake or sleep, we should live together with Him" (1 Thessalonians 5:9–10).

14. "This is a faithful saying and worthy of all acceptance, that Christ Jesus came into the world to save sinners, of whom I am chief" (1 Timothy 1:15).

15. "And this is the testimony: that God has given us eternal life, and this life is in His Son. He who has the Son has life; and he who does not have the Son of God does not have life" (1 John 5:11–12).

LAST WORDS, FIRST STEPS

Chapter 2 Discussion Questions

1. Why was the Savior crucified between two thieves?

2. Why wasn't the first thief's prayer for deliverance answered?

3. What are the differences in the two thieves' attitudes and destinies?

4. Of all the people present at the scene of the cross, why did Christ save a lowly thief?

5. What good deeds must we perform to qualify for Christ's pardon?

6. Is it ever too late for someone to be saved by God's grace?

7. How does one receive the rich pardon of salvation offered by Jesus?

Woman, behold thy son! . . . disciple,
Behold thy mother!

—

John 19:26–27 KJV

CHAPTER 3

WOMAN, BEHOLD THY SON! . . . DISCIPLE, BEHOLD THY MOTHER!

WORD OF PATERNITY

On history's battlefields lies a sea of fallen warriors. They are diverse in rank and creed, age and ethnicity, cause and allegiance, yet equally bound together in death. And with their dying breath, their common last words often bind them together as well—the desperate cry, perhaps the anguish-filled moan, "Mother."

Whether it's a dying soldier or a death-row inmate, the last words are almost always a call for mother. She holds a special place in her son's heart.

Yet as Jesus dies, His last words addressing His mother are divinely different. In the crucible of His greatest suffering, this Son does not call out to His mother for comfort and relief. Rather, He comes to her aid and bears her pain with paternal words of comfort and blessing.

Social Justice and the Church

Care for the widow and orphan is directed from Christ Himself at His darkest moment. More than forty Scripture verses compel compassion for these most vulnerable among us. So where's the social justice in the church today? This question is one of the most controversial topics I've encountered as a talk show host.

Social justice has become a hot topic in the church. Is it because of political groups that claim to love the poor under the guise of social justice but loathe the things of God? Is it because the church is often accused of the opposite—being pious and heavenly minded—while neglecting the needy ones here on earth? We use spiritual-sounding clichés like, "If the church would only perform her God-given role, there would be no need for government welfare programs."

Why does the Body of Christ so often fail to act as a body? Let's look at the answer to these questions, not from the perspective of a political party, club, or group—but straight from the Cross.

Widows and Orphans

Pestilence, wars, famine, and death are widow makers. Add to the list accidental death, sickness, disease, and the fact that women on average outlive men, and you begin to understand the enormity and burden of widowhood.

In many nations a widow is despised and looked down upon. Property can be taken from her and given to male heirs, leaving her destitute. Historians write that the wife of Abraham Lincoln, Mary Todd Lincoln, was left so impoverished after his assassination that she was unable to maintain the family home. Desperate and facing the prospect of having to live on charity, she lobbied Congress for years in an effort to receive a stipend based on her husband's service and ultimate sacrifice for his country. But the harder she tried to get her husband's meager pension, the more resistance she encountered because a woman who engaged in politics was viewed as unseemly. It wasn't until shortly before her death that Congress approved a livable pension for her.[1]

No other group is more affected by the sin of omission than the widows of today. Therefore, it is not surprising that even in the moment of His greatest crisis Jesus continued to display uninterrupted compassion for Mary, the neglected, and all the widows of Jerusalem and beyond.

Pure and undefiled religion before God and the Father is this: to visit orphans and widows in their trouble, and to keep oneself unspotted from the world. (James 1:27)

Jesus was equally concerned for the fatherless and orphans. He had a very special place in His heart for "the least of these" (Matthew 25:40). Sadly, 5,760 children worldwide become orphans every day. The United Nations Children's Fund (UNICEF) reports that there are between 143 million and 210 million orphans worldwide.[2] Many fall victim to child trafficking, sex slavery, and other unspeakable evils.

Obedient unto the Cross, even as He ignominiously and painfully hung there, Jesus never wavered in His determination to accomplish His mission.

He first addresses His Father and second, the thief. He then shifts His focus to His mother and the apostle John. Together, these four figures represent all categories and people in time and history.

- *His heavenly Father:* the One who commissioned Him from eternity
- *The thief:* an emblem of fallen humanity, for whom He died

- *His mother*: the earthly vessel through whom God incarnated His Son to save the lost
- *His apostle*: a key representative of the Body of Christ—the church

In a real sense, Mary and John represent the plight of widows and orphans in need of divine care, though we can't be certain of their actual social status.

Amid His own pain and suffering, Jesus cares for *Mary's* pain and suffering. Here hangs the only Son who has ever fully understood His mother's anguish. A certain weight, if not double grief, now afflicts the Man of Sorrows. He feels empathy for His mother's intense suffering and future, as well as a far deeper sorrow for her innate sinfulness as one counted among the fallen seed of Adam.

As Jesus sees Mary standing there, He speaks to her directly and says . . .

"Woman, Behold Thy Son"

Profound and unrelenting grief awaits the mother who loses a son. It's often said, "No parent should have to bury their own child." Imagine the pain Mary was forced to endure, watching her son die—and the most brutal of deaths. Yet God's invisible hand was at work. Miraculously, while Jesus' physical body was being torn, His spiritual body was being formed right there in front of Him.

So why does Jesus address Mary as "woman" and not the more tender word *mother*? Perhaps in this reference Jesus intentionally transfers the priority from her position as His mother to that of a lost soul in need of a Savior. Or maybe the Savior knew the further pain that would be inflicted if He referred to her as "mother," evoking deep maternal sympathy.

Another perspective from R. C. Sproul examines the actual word Jesus used in the original language, highlighting the intimate bond between Jesus and Mary. In his commentary on John, he explains this perplexing word choice:

> There is something in the original Greek here that I find very special, very touching. Jesus addressed His mother *"Woman,"* and that sounds somewhat impersonal and disrespectful to our ears. But the word that Jesus used in the Greek is *gone*, from which we get our word *gynecology*. This was the universal term for "woman," but it also was used frequently as an honorific title of endearment. When Jesus addressed His mother as "Woman," He was using a term of tenderness. He used this same term when He spoke to His mother at the wedding feast in Cana (John 2:4) and He also used it to address the woman caught in

adultery (John 8:10); in the midst of her shame and embarrassment, He spoke to her with tenderness. This is a side of our Savior we need to see—He was tender and respectful toward His mother and other women.[3]

From a Wooden Trough to a Wooden Cross

What a stark contrast we find between the Mary of Bethlehem and the Mary at the Cross. "Round yon virgin" and "Sleep in heavenly peace"[4] give way to devastating darkness here at Golgotha.

The unique calling of the Mary at the Cross and the depth of her heartbreak are unsurpassed. The One she bore some thirty-three years earlier now bears the burden of her own sin and that of the whole world, as she watches His bloodied body hang on the Tree of Death. She who had delivered Him was being delivered by Him. The fruit of her womb becomes the Firstfruits of all creation.

Perhaps Mary reflects back on those moments at the manger we now sing about at Christmas:

> *What child is this, who, laid to rest,*
> *On Mary's lap is sleeping?*
> *Whom angels greet with anthems sweet,*
> *While shepherds watch are keeping?*

This, this is Christ the King,
Whom shepherds guard and angels sing:
Haste, haste to bring Him laud,
The babe, the son of Mary.[5]

Jesus' death displays a son and mother united under the same Father. How significant that the God-man hangs as mediator between His heavenly Father and His earthly mother. Mary's eldest heir dies to make her one of the "joint heirs with Christ" (Romans 8:17). Because the Son *dies,* the mother *lives* to become a daughter of the Father, who sent His Son to be the Savior.

Thanks to these paternal words spoken by Jesus, the family is about to grow even more. Motherly love can only watch helplessly, unable to intervene, as Jesus' divine love takes action. The death of her firstborn son now gives rise to another son born spiritually out of that same death.

In His selfless and dying state, Jesus now calls upon His mother to take on another as her son. He commits her into John's care with the words . . .

"Behold Thy Mother!"

How many mothers have lost and gained a son in the same day? In an instant the weight of Simeon's prophetic words in Luke 2:35 struck Mary's heart: "Yes, a sword will pierce through your own soul also." Mary *lost* a son who died to save the *lost*. Now, while dying, He gives her another son who will lead many *lost* to salvation. Jesus also perfectly fulfills the Fifth Commandment (Exodus 20:12) by honoring His heavenly Father (John 17:4) and His earthly mother in perfect unison.

But why John? He was the only one of the disciples who had not fled the scene of the crucifixion. Perhaps his singular presence at his Master's death showed the depth of courage needed to fulfill the commission of caring for Mary. As he stands by Jesus in His death, John now becomes Mary's son, to stand by her in her final days. Through eyes of anguished pain, Jesus sees one lone disciple there by His mother—His beloved disciple who no doubt risked it all just to be near his Lord at this moment. As Christ fulfills His Levitical role as firstborn son to dispatch care for His mother, so John fulfills his role as a "born again" son in his care for the widow.

John Calvin writes that it's as though Christ is saying, "Henceforth, I shall not be an inhabitant of the earth, so as to have it in my power to discharge to thee the duties of . . . a son; and therefore, I put this man in my room, that he may perform my office."[6]

In His greatest moment of extreme agony we watch our Lord care for the widow and orphan. When all is taken from Him, He keeps on giving, even to those who were there to minister to Him. "The Son of Man did not come to be served" (Matthew 20:28) but was selfless to the end, perfectly displaying "greater love has no one than this" (John 15:13). The last words spoken by Jesus to any human before His death were to these two whom He loved.

Andrew of Crete, an eighth-century martyr, urges us:

> Let us say to Christ: *Blessed is he who comes in the name of the Lord*, the king of Israel. Let us wave before him like palm branches the words inscribed above him on the cross. Let us show him honor, not with olive branches, but with the splendor of merciful deeds to one another. Let us spread the thoughts and desires of our hearts under his feet like garments, so that he may draw the whole of our being into himself and place the whole of his in us.[7]

Care to the End

In divine orchestration, as the Head is being killed, the Body is being born. Witness the earthly uniting of mother and son just moments before the heavenly separation of Father and Son. See the great care with which Jesus Christ connects His earthly family as He enters into a greater work of redemption on behalf of his greater Body—the redeemed of God.

How providential is the uniting of these two! Mary was the first to look into Christ's eyes in the little town of Bethlehem, and John the Apostle will be the last to gaze into eyes that were "like a flame of fire" on the isle of Patmos (Revelation 1:14).

Arthur W. Pink notes that, years later, Jesus would reveal Himself to the apostle John on the isle of Patmos. How appropriate that Jesus prepared John for this future event by placing him alongside the woman who had lived in closest intimacy and fellowship with Him on earth! Pink observes, "We can therefore see that there was a significant appropriateness to bringing these two—Mary and John—together. Admire, then, the prudence of Christ's election of a home for Mary, and at the same time providing a companion for the disciple whom He loved with whom He might have blessed spiritual fellowship."[8]

The fruit of John's ministry to Mary has impacted the body of Christ since the beginning of the church. Are we ministering to the widows, the orphans, and those in need among us?

Recently I was discouraged when my pastor shared that as many as 80 percent of church members are *not* actually involved in church ministry.[9] In fact, 95 percent of Christians, according to one study, will never share the life-changing message of the gospel in their lifetime. Worse yet, fewer than 10 percent of American Christians feel any obligation to share their faith.[10]

Where Is the Body of Christ?

A great example to all of us is my own father, who is passionate about reaching the fatherless in our culture. In fact, he carried such a burden that he helped launch a national nonprofit, The Christian Association of Youth Mentoring. Multiple times a week he pulls his big SUV into a Section 8 housing complex on the east side of Winston-Salem. From there he mentors several boys as well as helps young mothers without husbands. The conspicuously missing component in this small community is fathers.

According to the US Census Bureau, twenty-four million children in America, or one out of three, live in biological-father-absent homes. Children in father-absent homes are almost four times more likely to be poor.[11] Youths who never had a father in the household experienced the highest odds.[12] One study showed that as many as 85 percent of youths in prison grew up in fatherless homes.[13] My father is fond of saying, "Why curse the darkness, when you can light a candle?"

How are you being the Body of Christ to fatherless boys and girls in your church and community? When was the last time you spent just five minutes with a young person desperate for direction and coaching? Those five minutes could change a life. Or maybe it's time to get radically personal about foster care and adoption. We can be like those in David Platt's church in Birmingham, Alabama, who got serious about making a difference in their community and decided to adopt a significant number of orphans out of their state's foster care.[14]

Or maybe your church would be willing to adopt and impact some of the roughest public schools in your city. My friend Dr. Tony Evans did this in Dallas, Texas. When a local principal contacted Dr. Evans about his students' dire need for tough love and accountability, Dr. Evans and his church launched The Turn-Around Agenda. To date, this outreach has adopted seventy-three Dallas-area public schools to meet the critical needs of these urban youth.[15]

Christ's Hands and Feet

Don't miss Christ's message of social justice as He spoke this paternal Word of Life from the Tree of Death. You may never know, on this side of eternity, the level of impact you can have, even on a radio program—just ask the "Christian Car Guy," Robby Dilmore.

"Are y'all tellin' me that you talk about Jesus Christ on the radio?" the incredulous auto repair shop owner said in a classic Texas drawl. He had answered a call from Robby

Dilmore, host of the radio program, *The Christian Car Guy*. Robby challenges the church and Christian-owned auto repair shops to provide free car repair labor to single mothers and widows through a feature called "Jesus' Labor of Love." Hundreds have been helped.

Robby called this Texan because of a request from a woman in Fort Worth. Her car was wrecked and sitting in her driveway. The front end was so severely damaged, the wheels wouldn't turn and the battery was crushed. She needed a battery just to find out if her car would start.

Robby explained to the man the extent of the repair. "I will never forget his response," Robby recalls. "He said, 'You know, son, there are things a lot more important than money. I'll go to that lady's house and I'll have her on the road today!'"

Another rescue had an element of humor in it. A woman in North Carolina had been suffering for two years with an air conditioner in her car that she could not get working, and it was blistering hot one summer day. Listening to *Jesus' Labor of Love*, she called in to see if she could get help from one of the auto-repair partners. With address in hand she drove to the shop, enduring the suffocating heat. Thankfully, the mechanic took a look at the problem and was able to fix it. "Ma'am, see that little button there with the snowflake on it? That turns on your air conditioning."[16]

Are you engaged in true Christ-based, Cross-based social justice? Is your church actively serving the widow and orphan? Jesus paid it all on the Cross. The Body of Christ is the Church. We are Christ's hands and feet. Sometimes all Jesus requires of us is just a willing finger to push a button!

Thus the Nazarene speaks these words . . .

Woman, behold thy son!
Disciple, behold thy mother!

We see a divinely orchestrated adoption take place at this bloody scene.

We'll see the reality of divine adoption made possible with His next Word of Life from the Tree of Death.

SCRIPTURAL REFLECTIONS ON THE LAST WORDS OF JESUS

Woman, Behold Thy Son! . . .
Disciple, Behold Thy Mother!

1. "Honor your father and your mother, that your days might be long upon the land which the LORD your God is giving you" (Exodus 20:12).

2. "A father of the fatherless, a defender of widows, is God in His holy habitation" (Psalm 68:5).

3. "Learn to do good, seek justice, rebuke the oppressor; defend the fatherless, plead for the widow" (Isaiah 1:17).

4. "The Spirit of the LORD God is upon Me, because the LORD has anointed Me to preach good tidings to the poor; He has sent Me to heal the brokenhearted, to proclaim liberty to the captives, and the opening of the prison to those who are bound; to proclaim the acceptable year of the LORD, and the day of vengeance of our God; to comfort all who mourn, to console those who mourn in Zion, to give them beauty for ashes, the oil of joy for mourning, the garment of praise for the spirit of heaviness; that they might be called trees of righteous-

ness, the planting of the LORD, that He may be glorified" (Isaiah 61:1–3).

5. "Leave your fatherless children, I will preserve them alive; and let your widows trust in Me" (Jeremiah 49:11).

6. "Now there stood by the cross of Jesus His mother, and His mother's sister, Mary the wife of Clopas, and Mary Magdalene" (John 19:25).

7. "Now in those days, when the number of the disciples was multiplying, there arose a complaint against the Hebrews by the Hellenists, because their widows were neglected in the daily distribution" (Acts 6:1).

8. "Therefore, brethren, seek out from among you seven men of good reputation, full of the Holy Spirit and wisdom, whom we may appoint over this business" (Acts 6:3).

9. "But when the fullness of the time had come, God sent forth His Son, born of a woman, born under the law, to redeem those who were under the law, that we might receive the adoption as sons" (Galatians 4:4–5).

10. "But [we], speaking the truth in love, may grow up in all things into Him who is the head—Christ—from whom

the whole body, joined and knit together by what every joint supplies, according to the effective working by which every part does its share, causes growth of the body for the edifying of itself in love" (Ephesians 4:15–16).

11. "For we are members of His body, of His flesh and of His bones" (Ephesians 5:30).

12. "And He is the head of the body, the church, who is the beginning, the firstborn from the dead; that in all things He may have the preeminence. For it pleased the Father that in Him all the fullness should dwell, and by Him to reconcile all things to Himself, by Him, whether things on earth or things in heaven, having made peace through the blood of His cross" (Colossians 1:18–20).

13. "Honor widows who are really widows" (1 Timothy 5:3).

14. "Pure and undefiled religion before God and the Father is this: to visit orphans and widows in their trouble, and to keep oneself unspotted from the world" (James 1:27).

15. "By this we know love, because He laid down His life for us. And we also ought to lay down our lives for the brethren" (1 John 3:16).

LAST WORDS, FIRST STEPS

Chapter 3 Discussion Questions

1. What are you most moved by as you consider Mary's pain in watching her son suffer such a horrendous death?

2. Why would Jesus, in such a moment of crisis, offer comfort to Mary and John?

3. How well is the church currently performing her role as the "Body of Christ" to our suffering and needy world?

4. Why should the church be more engaged in true social justice?

5. How is your church serving the widows, orphans, and fatherless children in your community?

6. If you are a believer, what is your spiritual gift—and how are you serving the Body of Christ with your gift?

7. What first steps do these words of Jesus inspire you to take regarding your involvement with helping others in need?

My God, my God,
why hast thou forsaken me?

—

Matthew 27:46; Mark 15:34 KJV

MY GOD, MY GOD, WHY HAST THOU FORSAKEN ME?

WORD OF PAIN

Frightened twelve-year-old Gregory has been prepped for surgery to remove a lemon-sized tumor embedded in the base of his brain. As he is wheeled on a gurney bound for the surgeon's knife, he tightly grasps his father's hand. Because of the tumor's dangerous location, doctors determined that surgical removal of the entire growth could cause partial paralysis. With chemotherapy prescribed after surgery, it's everyone's hope and prayer that the remaining tumor will shrink, sparing his life, but there are no guarantees. The orderlies whisk him down the long hospital hallway. Blazing light after blazing light passes above him as his father reassures him that everything will be all right. His father's soft words penetrate the darkness of fear: "I love you, son. Everything will be okay. I'm here for you. I'll be waiting."

The boy loves his dad deeply. They do everything together and have never been apart. The thought of being separated from his father—or worse, never seeing him again—is devastating. As the door opens to the surgery room, the most horrible moment arrives, *greater* than the physical pain of the cancerous tumor besieging his body. The young boy must let go of his father's hand. He must walk through the valley of the shadow of death alone.

The father can only watch and wait from a distance. His heart is broken with anguish as he releases his son's hand.

The son now faces the biggest challenge of his existence. For what will seem like an eternity, life and death will hang in the balance.

The importance of a father in a child's life cannot be overstated. Yet tragically today, gaping father wounds are everywhere in our society, where millions of kids grow up without a dad. Thousands more have dads who are present but have forsaken them emotionally. Father wounds are just one of the many wounds absorbed by Jesus on this first Good Friday.

Enter one of the greatest mysteries in all of history. In the garden, the first Adam forsook God. On the Cross, the second Adam is forsaken by God to redeem for Himself the fallen sons of Adam. However, this Father's forsaking was not one of unfaithfulness but of justice and to accomplish a greater purpose. Additionally, the second Adam took on the first Adam's nakedness and shame so Adam's fallen seed could one day be redeemed, clothed in righteousness, and greatly esteemed.

Of all Jesus' seven recorded Last Words from the Cross, the fourth Word is most perplexing and mysterious. This profound statement of Christ has confounded even the greatest of theologians.

The scene at the Cross now dramatically changes into darkness—dreadful darkness for three hours in the middle of the day (Matthew 27:45; Mark 15:33). As one writer put it, "By a miraculous act of Almighty God, midday becomes midnight."[1] All the experts agree, the sixth hour would have been twelve noon. After three hours of hanging on the Tree of Death at the height of the Passover sacrifice, the Lamb of God is encompassed by a veil of darkness. When the sun is supposed to shine at its brightest, the Son is enveloped by night.

Well might the sun and darkness hide
And shut his glories in
When Christ, the mighty Maker died
For man the creature's sin.[2]

"My God, My God"

This is the only time Christ ever addressed the Father this way. But why? These words mark a graphic departure from other prayers the Son of God had prayed.

Yet in this messianic fulfillment of Psalm 22, the Lord continues to demonstrate intimacy with two exclamations of the simple possessive pronoun "My." God was still "His" God who had commissioned the "Beloved One" to be bruised and suffer greatly.

Jesus' suffering was so unfathomable mentally, physically, and spiritually and that it was summed up in the form of the question . . .

"Why"

Christ encounters all of the pain here in this darkness. In His plaintive cry to His Father, we see perhaps the biggest *why* ever asked. Each person confronted with the knowledge of these events is challenged by the question, *Why?* Why did this happen? Why did this happen the way it did? Why would God pour out His wrath on the Innocent One? Why would

God, who is perfect in all His attributes, forsake His Son for all eternity at this point? Is He an unfaithful Father, or is there a greater purpose, mission, and cause behind it all?

Ultimately it is at the foot of the Cross that all *why* questions find their answer. Why do people suffer? Why do bad things happen to good people? Job and his friends asked, "Why?" Throughout the ages even mature believers have asked, "Why?"

It's fascinating that here we have the one occasion in history where *God* is asking *God*, "Why?"

The answer comes in the form of God's lightning bolts of judgment aimed at the One of whom Pontius Pilate proclaimed, "I find no fault in this Man" (Luke 23:4). Yet the *why* questions continue as Almighty God pours out His wrath. The judgment of the Day of the Lord is unfurled upon all perversions of the worst sort—lust, greed, torture, pride, deceit, rape, divorce, abuse, immorality, pedophilia, racism, adultery, homosexuality, idolatry, hate, suicide, abortion, theft—and every imaginable vice of thought, word, or action, including all rebellion and shame! All aimed at the Savior, who "knew no sin" but became "sin for us" (2 Corinthians 5:21).

This was the *only* occasion in history where *bad* things happened to *good* people—actually the only *good* Person.

John R. W. Stott asserts, "The cross does not solve the

problem of suffering, but it supplies the essential perspective from which to look at it."[3]

"Hast Thou Forsaken Me?"

"He is despised and rejected by men" (Isaiah 53:3). Yes, Jesus was forsaken by His followers, friends, fans, and family. This, however, in no way compares to the infinite pain of feeling forsaken by His Father. Jesus endures public retribution from the same Father who had publicly declared,

You are My beloved Son, in whom I am well pleased. (Mark 1:11)

Here we see a momentary tension in the most intimate of relationships spanning all eternity: past, present, and future. Yet in that moment, Jesus never ceased to be God—a mystery indeed! The Savior absorbed the wrath of Almighty God due unjust sinners while never ceasing to be fully God at the same time.

The Son was *forsaken* to make possible the *fulfillment* of His other Words of Life:

- *Forsaken* so the Father could forgive them.
- *Forsaken* so He could be united with the repentant in paradise.

- *Forsaken* so the widow and orphan could be accepted and adopted.

- *Forsaken* so judgment might be rendered and sins atoned.

- *Forsaken* to endure unspeakable physical agony on the Cross.

- *Forsaken* so His work would be finished.

- *Forsaken* so He could ultimately commit His spirit to and be reunited with His Father.

The Darkest of Days

Observe the Cross, where *all* the darkness—separation, rejection, wrath, and hell—aimed like an arrow at the heart of sinners, is now fully absorbed by the Friend of Sinners. The Light of the World hangs abandoned, immersed in a world of darkness.

F. W. Krummacher describes this scene: "The Lord withdrew himself from the eyes of men behind the black curtain of appalling night, as behind the thick veil of the temple. He hung there a full three hours on the Cross, His thorn-crowned head thoughtfully drooping on his breast, involved in that darkness. He is in the most holy place. He stands at the altar of the Lord. He performs his sacrificial functions. He is the true Aaron, and at the same time, the Lamb."[4]

In the darkness of our souls we arrive at this horrific scene. When His eyes of fire pierce your heart, what will the Holy One encounter? Consider for a moment your most evil thought or deed. That thing you've never even shared with those closest to you. Are you prepared to face a holy God on the Day of Judgment?

What punishment do you deserve for this? How do you think your sins will be remedied?

How many of your sins did Jesus suffer for? *All of them!*

Surrounded and pressed upon by the darkness, Jesus Christ does His greatest work as mediator—standing between a holy God and sinful people. He took my place in hell and suffering in that moment—and not just mine, but the place of all lost sinners. *Our whipping! Our punishment!* As a perfect substitute, Jesus took on Himself the just punishment deserved by others.

The punishment due for all our sin and shame is absorbed by the Innocent One in that moment! Jesus dies, "the just for the unjust, that He might bring us to God" (1 Peter 3:18).

Alan D. Wright addresses how in this moment Christ not only bore every sin ever committed, but He also bore all the shame associated with them: "On the cross, Jesus Christ was not only bearing the sin of the child molester, He also was bearing the shame of the bewildered, broken child. He was not only bearing the sin of the prostitute's adultery, He was bearing the shame of the prostitute's identity as well. He not only was bearing the sin of the alcoholic's drunkenness, but at the same time, was bearing the shame of the alcoholic's child who never invited friends home to play. And Jesus took the shame willingly."[5]

The darkness of sin was dealt with head on in the darkness of Golgotha. Redemption can be offered for the worst sin because Jesus directly bore the sins here, suffering the Father's wrath upon sin. On the Tree of Death, the "Lamb of God who takes away the sin of the world" lays down His life (John 1:29).

So after the three darkest, most grueling hours of incomprehensible hell ever suffered, Jesus quotes the Psalmist: "Eli, Eli, lama sabachthani" ("My God, My God, why have You forsaken Me?" [Psalm 22:1]). These are the only words Jesus speaks to characterize the three hours of darkness.

It is said that Martin Luther agonized over these words to the point of fasting and prostrate silence. He came out of his meditation with the proclamation, "God forsaken by God, how can this be?"

Dr. Erwin Lutzer says of those three hours: "Jesus was a sacrifice for many people, so he had to compress an eternity of hell into three hours. As best we can, we must grasp that this was infinite suffering for the infinite Son of God. . . .

Look at these three hours on the Cross and you are looking into hell—darkness, loneliness, and abandonment by God."[6]

Only because of such darkness in the middle of the day can we triumphantly sing, "At the cross where I first saw the light."[7]

"Good News" from Isaiah

Pray and ponder these words from the prophet Isaiah, spoken nearly seven hundred years before the Cross and recorded in the book of Isaiah, also known as the "Gospel of the Old Testament":

> He is despised and rejected by men, a Man of sorrows and acquainted with grief. And we hid, as it were, our faces from Him; He was despised, and we did not esteem Him. Surely He has borne our griefs and carried our sorrows; yet we esteemed Him stricken, smitten by God, and afflicted. But He was wounded for our transgressions, He was bruised for our iniquities; the chastisement for our peace was upon Him, and by His stripes we are healed. All we like sheep have gone astray; we have turned, every one, to his own way; and the LORD has laid on Him the iniquity of us all.
>
> He was oppressed and He was afflicted, yet He

opened not His mouth; He was led as a lamb to the slaughter, and as a sheep before its shearers is silent, so He opened not His mouth. He was taken from prison and from judgment, and who will declare His generation? For He was cut off from the land of the living; for the transgressions of My people He was stricken. (Isaiah 53:3–8)

No greater pain has ever been experienced on any level than the hell of Christ suffering in this moment. But why? Because He carried *all* of that pain, sin, guilt, and shame in that moment. Yet on a far deeper level He was forsaken and punished for us to reconcile us to God (2 Corinthians 5:18).

Tim Keller illustrates it this way:

If after a service some Sunday morning one of the members of my church comes to me and says, "I never want to see you or talk to you again," I will feel pretty bad. But if today my wife comes up to me and says, "I never want to see you or talk to you again," that's a lot worse. The longer the love, the deeper the love, the greater the torment of its loss.

But this forsakenness, this loss, was between the Father and the Son, who had loved each other from all eternity. . . .

Jesus, the Maker of the world, was being un-made. Why? Jesus was experiencing Judgment Day. "My God, my God, why have you forsaken me?" It wasn't a rhetorical question. And the answer is: *For you, for me, for us.*

Jesus was forsaken by God so that we would never have to be. The judgment that should have fallen on us fell instead on Jesus.[8]

Three hours of an unfathom'd pain,
Of drops falling like summer rain,
Earth's sympathy and heaven's eclipse—
Three hours the pale and dying lips
By their mysterious silence teach
Things far more beautiful than speech
In depth or height can ever reach.[9]

After many hours, a tired surgeon walks into the waiting room. Gregory's father and mother, hands intertwined, have been praying unceasingly. "We were able to remove it all," the doctor reports.

This young man was reunited with his father after his successful surgery. The outcome of this story has an ending filled with hope. A young life is spared and the bond between father and son remains unbroken. To this day, Gregory is visibly shaken when he recounts the moment he was separated from his father. Have you been reconciled with your heavenly Father? Do you understand the price that was paid to bring you back to the Father?

How profound it is that the greatest punishment of *divine* suffering was shielded from our eyes in those three hours of darkness. Yet the greatest pain of *human* suffering was laid bare in broad daylight for the whole world to see its bloody spectacle. While His divine suffering was far more mysterious, Christ's human suffering, as we'll see next, was certainly more tangible and graphic to the human eye.

SCRIPTURAL REFLECTIONS
ON THE LAST WORDS OF JESUS

My God, My God, Why Hast Thou Forsaken Me?

1. "The secret things belong to the LORD our God" (Deuteronomy 29:29).

2. "My God, My God, why have You forsaken Me? Why are You so far from helping Me, and from the words of My groaning?" (Psalm 22:1).

3. "My loved ones and my friends stand aloof from my plague, and my relatives stand afar off" (Psalm 38:11).

4. "You have put away my acquaintances far from me; You have made me an abomination to them; I am shut up, and I cannot get out" (Psalm 88:8).

5. "It is the glory of God to conceal a matter" (Proverbs 25:2).

6. "The people who walked in darkness have seen a great light; those who dwelt in the land of the shadow of death, upon them a light has shined" (Isaiah 9:2).

7. "Yet it pleased the LORD to bruise Him; He has put Him to grief" (Isaiah 53:10).

8. "Arise, shine; for your light has come! And the glory of the LORD is risen upon you. For behold, the darkness shall cover the earth, and deep darkness the people; but the LORD will arise over you, and His glory will be seen upon you. The Gentiles shall come to your light, and kings to the brightness of your rising" (Isaiah 60:1–3).

9. "'And it shall come to pass in that day,' says the Lord GOD, 'that I will make the sun go down at noon, and I will darken the earth in broad daylight'" (Amos 8:9).

10. "Now from the sixth hour until the ninth hour there was darkness over all the land. And about the ninth hour Jesus cried out with a loud voice saying, 'Eli, Eli, lama sabachthani?' that is, 'My God, My God, why have You forsaken Me?'" (Matthew 27:45–46)

11. "Now when the sixth hour had come, there was darkness over the whole land until the ninth hour. And at the ninth hour Jesus cried out with a loud voice, saying, 'Eloi, Eloi, lama sabachthani?' which is translated, 'My God, My God, why have You forsaken Me?'" (Mark 15:33–34).

12. "Then Jesus spoke to them again, saying, 'I am the light of the world. He who follows me shall not walk in darkness, but have the light of life'" (John 8:12).

13. "For if by the one man's offense death reigned through the one, much more those who receive abundance of grace and of the gift of righteousness will reign in life through the One, Jesus Christ" (Romans 5:17).

14. "For since by man came death, by Man also came the resurrection of the dead. For as in Adam all die, even so in Christ all shall be made alive" (1 Corinthians 15:21–22).

15. "For He made Him who knew no sin to be sin for us, that we might become the righteousness of God in Him" (2 Corinthians 5:21).

16. "Christ has redeemed us from the curse of the law, having become a curse for us (for it is written, 'Cursed is everyone who hangs on a tree')" (Galatians 3:13).

17. "For there is one God and one Mediator between God and men, the Man Christ Jesus" (1 Timothy 2:5).

18. "For such a High Priest was fitting for us, who is holy, harmless, undefiled, separate from sinners, and has become higher than the heavens; who does not need daily, as those high priests, to offer up sacrifices, first for His own sins, and then for the people's, for this He did once for all when He offered up Himself" (Hebrews 7:26–27).

19. "Let your conduct be without covetousness; be content with such things as you have. For He Himself has said, 'I will never leave you nor forsake you'" (Hebrews 13:5).

20. "You were not redeemed with corruptible things, like silver or gold, from your aimless conduct received by tradition from your fathers, but with the precious blood of Christ, as of a lamb without blemish and without spot" (1 Peter 1:18–19).

LAST WORDS, FIRST STEPS

Chapter 4 Discussion Questions

1. Why were there three hours of darkness in the middle of the day?

2. Why are these words of Christ so deep and mysterious?

3. Is there anything in your past so dark and painful that it is outside of God's healing reach?

4. What does Jesus mean by *forsaken*?

5. Why was Christ's pain as expressed in these words more traumatic than even the physical pain He experienced?

6. What kind of shame do we experience because of our sin?

7. How was weight of sin and shame dealt with in this moment on the Cross?

I thirst.

—

John 19:28 KJV

I THIRST

WORD OF PASSION

It was Wednesday night at church in the fall of 1979. As a fun-loving fifth-grader I had no clue about the intense trauma I was about to experience. I'll never forget the moment I first heard the entire grisly account. Gathered in a poorly lit classroom with barely a dozen other boys, we hung on every word as the youth worker took us point by point through Christ's execution narrative. No goofing off, mimicking the teacher, passing notes, or making funny faces. Just a somber stillness entombed the classroom, as if we were right there at the scene of the Cross.

"Were You There When They Crucified My Lord?"
Can you call to mind the deep voice of Johnny Cash singing this age-old hymn?[1] When was the last time you were there—

at the Cross? When was the last time someone helped you envision the Savior's suffering from the time of His betrayal to His final breath?

Indeed, it is a place that's real. A place of cold, calculated, even celebrated torture.

Over the past two thousand years the Cross has been memorialized in classical and modern art, music, literature, and in recent times, film. Maybe you've seen the landmark movie *The Passion of the Christ.* Irrespective of the medium, the message of the Cross remains the same. It's an infamous place of brutal cruelty and savagery of the basest human degree. History reaches its most decisive climax on this barbarous and bloody ground.

Ultimately, it's a place we must visit. Those who journey there will never be the same! Redemptive history's trail of blood abruptly ends at Passover on a skull-shaped place outside Jerusalem.

Alan D. Wright notes:

The blood stream ran from the Passover lamb, to the altar of the tabernacle, to the sprinkled High Priest on the Day of Atonement. From His flogged flesh, to His thorn-pierced brow, to His nailed wrists, to His impaled side—the blood of Jesus flowed freely to cover your shame.[2]

"I Thirst"

Christ's physical pain on the Cross is summarized by "I thirst," the shortest translated of Jesus' seven Last Words. How instructive that the Suffering Servant utters such brief words about His own self at this ghastly scene.

Tens of thousands of people die every year of thirst, water deprivation, or waterborne diseases. According to the World Health Organization, every fifteen seconds a child dies from a preventable disease associated with lack of clean water.[3] I saw firsthand the critical importance of water when I traveled with a team to Darfur, Sudan. We were overwhelmed at the life-saving impact of the water wells our Truth Network listeners supported—saving thousands of lives. Beforehand, the water they drank was so putrid you wouldn't wash your feet in it.[4]

Here, hanging on the brink of death, we hear the source of Living Water cry, "I thirst."

Having experienced an intense level of pain prior to His crucifixion, the Man of Sorrows must now endure a greater agony on the Tree of Death.

Yet the briefest of the seven Last Words on the Cross— "I thirst"—is the only statement in which Jesus refers to His physical discomfort. This fascinating little phrase summarizes much of what's commonly referred to as the Passion of the Christ.

Let's look closer at His tremendous suffering represented by the simple words, "I thirst"—the fifth Word of Life spoken by Jesus from the Tree of Death.

The Crowd

I never noticed an intriguing verse in Matthew's Gospel until more closely examining the details of Christ's death: "Sitting down, *they* kept watch over Him there" (Matthew 27:36). It's almost as though the first-century mob grabbed their chairs, tailgate gear, and ice chests, all ready to watch a big game.

Let us now, like the crowd on Calvary, sit and observe one of the cruelest forms of punishment imaginable: death by crucifixion. Hank Hanegraaff puts into context this method of execution: "The Lord experienced ultimate physical torture in the form of the cross. The Roman system of crucifixion had been fine-tuned to produce maximum pain."[5]

Witnessing something of such historic magnitude will most certainly impact our perspective on life, death, pain, and reality forever. Here we'll see the same rite of execution about which the Roman philosopher Cicero once stated nearly five decades before Jesus' death on the cross: "No word can be found to describe so monstrous a proceeding."[6]

The spectacle began after a sleepless but intense night of the Passover feast, also known as the Last Supper, and prayer in the Garden of the Gethsemane. Now what follows is the time for His literal body and blood to be broken and poured out. In the early hours before dawn, Christ is betrayed by one of His own disciples, Judas Iscariot, who delivered Him into the hands of the soldiers and Jewish religious leaders.

So when Matthew 27:36 says, "Sitting down, *they* kept watch over Him there," let's back up and, using Matthew's eyewitness account, help identify who "they" are:

- *They* seized Him (Matthew 26:50).
- *They* took Him into a kangaroo court fraught with hired false accusers only to subject the Innocent One to more abuse (Matthew 26:59–60).
- *They* bound Him and led Him away (Matthew 27:2).
- Because of *their* bloodthirsty clamoring for His crucifixion, Pilate had Him flogged (Matthew 27:25–26).
- *They* stripped Him and put on Him a scarlet robe (Matthew 27:28).
- *They* pressed a crown of thorns upon His head, and a reed in His hand (Matthew 27:29).

R. C. Sproul points out that the crown of thorns would have caused Jesus great physical agony. "The thorns that were woven together to make this crown were spikes that reached a length of twelve inches. Then the whole of the mass of thorns was shoved down on Jesus' head so that the thorns were driven into His temples, all for the sport of the soldiers."[7]

> *O sacred head now wounded,*
> *with grief and shame way down,*
> *now scornfully surrounded*
> *with thorns thine Only crown.*[8]

- *They* bowed before him and mocked him (Matthew 27:29).
- *They* spat on Him (Matthew 27:30).
- *They* took the reed and struck Him on the head (Matthew 27:30).

The word "struck"—or "smote," in the King James Version of Matthew 27:30—could be synonymous for *hit, attacked, smacked, punched, mugged, blindsided.* All the while, He was being viciously mocked, cursed, laughed at, and abused (Matthew 27:31).

Following the farcical trial packed with false witnesses against Jesus—first Herod, then Pilate, then Herod and Pilate again, in several verses before and after Matthew 27:36, we are told in sickening detail what *they* did to Him.

But who are *they*?

- The soldiers?
- The mob?
- The religious leaders?
- The people?
- Herod?
- Pilate?

The answer is yes! All of the above participated as *they* in that darkest of days. And *they* continued their assault on the Son of God all the way to the Tree of Death.

- "When *they* had mocked Him, *they* took the robe off Him" (Matthew 27:31).
- "[Simon of Cyrene] *they* compelled to bear His cross" (Matthew 27:32).
- "*They* gave Him sour wine mingled with gall to drink" (Matthew 27:34).
- "*They* crucified Him" (Matthew 27:35).
- "*They* . . . divided His garments, casting lots" (Matthew 27:35).
- "Sitting down, *they* kept watch over Him there" (Matthew 27:36).
- "*They* that passed by reviled him, wagging their heads" (Matthew 27:39 KJV).

The Scourging

Before bearing the weight of the heavy, splintered cross beam, Christ's back was severely lacerated by professional soldiers using the infamous cat-o'-nine-tails.

In his book *The Case for Christ,* forensic journalist Lee Strobel describes the horrific method of scourging. The soldiers would braid leather thongs into a whip and then weave metal balls and sharp bone fragments into it. As a result of this whipping, Strobel says, "The back would be so shredded that part of the spine was sometimes exposed by the deep, deep cuts. The whipping would have gone all the way from the shoulders down to the back, the buttocks, and the backs of the legs. It was just terrible."[9]

Christ's condition, no doubt, was a fulfillment of the prophet Isaiah's words centuries earlier: "His visage was marred more than any man, and His form more than the sons of men" (Isaiah 52:14).

According to Greg Laurie, "Scourging was so barbaric they called it the 'half-way' death, because it would tear the skin from the back as it would expose the bones and the vital organs."[10]

The Journey

We know Jesus survived the flogging, but things only got worse from there. The heavy Cross was then laid upon His wounded back. The most difficult journey lay just ahead. The renowned Via Dolorosa, or "Journey of Grief," runs through a narrow road in Jerusalem to Golgotha.

> *And He, bearing His cross, went out to a place called the Place of a Skull, which is called in Hebrew, Golgotha.* (John 19:17)

Writhing in pain and most likely experiencing extreme faintness from severe bleeding or hypovolemic shock,[11] Jesus fell. At that moment Simon the Cyrene was appointed to carry the Cross the remaining distance (Luke 23:26). Enduring inconceivable physical duress, is it any wonder that Jesus was thirsty?

Max Lucado describes the Innocent Prisoner's condition during the last lingering stages of His cruel and unjust execution:

Jesus. Lips cracked and mouth of cotton. Throat so dry he couldn't swallow, and voice so hoarse he could scarcely speak. He is thirsty. . . .

Before the nail was pounded, a drink was offered. Mark says the wine was mixed with myrrh. Matthew described it as wine mixed with gall. Both myrrh and gall contain sedative properties that numb the senses. But Jesus refused them. He refused to be stupefied by the drugs, opting instead to feel the full force of his suffering.[12]

The Nails

At the scene of the execution, things turn even more brutal. Take the largest nail and largest hammer you can find and imagine it being driven through your wrists and ankles. The Galilean Carpenter's hands, which once *drove* nails through wood, are now having nails *driven* through them.

The spikes driven into Jesus' wrists were five to seven inches long and tapered to a sharp point. "The nail would go through the place where the median nerve runs," Strobel says. "This is the largest nerve going out to the hand, and it would be crushed by the nail that was being pounded in."[13]

The pain would be extreme, absolutely unbearable. In fact, says Strobel, the pain "was literally beyond words to describe; they had to invent a new word: 'excruciating,' meaning 'out of the cross.' Note: they had to create a new word to describe the pain because nothing in the language could describe the intense anguish caused by the crucifixion."[14]

After the nails were driven into Jesus' wrists, the crossbar was attached to the vertical stake, His body was hoisted up, and then nails were driven through Jesus' feet. The nails would have crushed the nerves in His feet.

The Cross

While many accounts of the Savior's suffering gloss over these grisly details, one such detail requires notice. Imagine the trauma to Christ's extremities as He was roughly lifted up by the executioners into His final position, jerking and jarring every joint, ligament, and nerve in His anatomy. Now the new struggle of gasping for each breath ensues. Scholars widely agree that suffocation was a major part of suffering for crucifixion victims.

How often do we take each breath for granted? Yet for hours, Jesus was pushing up from His impaled feet with all His strength—for one breath of air.

The very One who breathed life into existence is now struggling desperately to breathe in life as death slowly envelops Him.

Hank Hanegraaff expounds upon this physical stress: "Breathing became an agonizing endeavor as Christ pushed His tortured body upward to grasp small gulps of air. In the ensuing hours He experienced cycles of joint-wrenching cramps, intermittent asphyxiation, and excruciating pain as His lacerated back moved up and down against the rough timber of the cross."[15]

Amazing love, how can it be?
That Thou my God shouldst die for me?[16]

Yet astonishingly and to His glory, with His last breaths on the Cross Jesus manages to speak Words of Life. When you consider the trauma of the Cross, it's amazing that only one of Jesus' seven recorded last words addressed His own physical pain. After as many as twenty-four hours without food or drink, compounded by the loss of blood and physical abuse—He uttered not one "cross" word from the Cross but only the brief expression, "I thirst." And this from the One who called blessed "those who thirst for righteousness" (Matthew 5:6).

Christ's enemies, however, were hell-bent to satisfy a darker thirst:

- Judas thirsted for money.
- Herod thirsted for power.
- Pilate thirsted for appeasement.
- The mob thirsted for blood.
- The soldiers thirsted for sport.
- The religious leaders thirsted for vengeance.

What do you thirst for? What are the deep needs in your heart, so secret that you dare tell no other human? The emptiness and pain inside of us creates shame, hurt, and despair. Only Jesus Christ can satisfy the deepest thirst of the human soul!

He who believes in Me shall never thirst. (John 6:35)

Here at this gruesome scene of Calvary, we have a Savior who displayed His nakedness and pain for the whole world to see. God provided animal skins to cover the shame and nakedness of the first Adam. But the second Adam had no such covering. Jesus hung there publicly—naked and shamed—so He could clothe the fallen sons of Adam in grace and righteousness. He alone who suffered openly for all to see can meet you in your darkest point of pain, where no one else can see.

His unthinkable shame can become your amazing gain! Alan D. Wright notes, "Father God allowed Jesus Christ to hang exposed and vulnerable, not only before the watching world but also before the whole invisible realm of spiritual powers. I believe that the mocking taunts of the Roman guards or passers-by held no comparison to the taunts of the invisible demons who were granted an unthinkable open season to shame the Son of God."[17]

In these brief words expressing Christ's passion, we see Him emptied out and thirsting, so lost sinners can be filled and made whole. In the depth of His passion of thirst, will you find satisfaction for your deepest hunger and thirst? The Cross of Christ is so much more than an ornate piece of jewelry. Yes, it's a symbol of death and destruction. But thankfully the cross is also a Tree of Life and a fountain of healing for those who find refuge in its shadow.

Take a moment and reflect on Jesus' suffering. Whether you're young as I was or near the end of your journey, take a seat next to "them" of Matthew 27:36 and watch Him there.[18]

> *See from his head, his hands, his feet,*
> *Sorrow and love flow mingled down!*
> *Did e'er such love and sorrow meet,*
> *Or thorns compose so rich a crown?*[19]

SCRIPTURAL REFLECTIONS
ON THE LAST WORDS OF JESUS

I Thirst

1. "But I am a worm, and no man; a reproach of men, and despised by the people. All those who see Me ridicule Me; they shoot out the lip, they shake the head, saying, 'He trusted in the LORD, let Him rescue Him; let Him deliver Him, since He delights in Him'" (Psalm 22:6–8).

2. "They gape at Me with their mouths, like a raging and a roaring lion. I am poured out like water, and all My bones are out of joint; My heart is like wax; it has melted within Me. My strength is dried up like a potsherd, and My tongue clings to My jaws; You have brought Me to the dust of death. For dogs have surrounded Me; the congregation of the wicked has enclosed me. They pierced My hands and My feet; I can count all my bones. They look and stare at me. They divide My garments among them, and for My clothing they cast lots" (Psalm 22:13–18).

3. "I am weary with my crying; my throat is dry; my eyes fail while I wait for my God" (Psalm 69:3).

4. "They gave me also gall for my food, and for my thirst they gave me vinegar to drink" (Psalm 69:21).

5. "I also have become a reproach to them; when they look at me, they shake their heads" (Psalm 109:25).

6. "For I will pour water on him who is thirsty, and floods on the dry ground; I will pour My Spirit on your descendants, and My blessing on your offspring" (Isaiah 44:3).

7. "I gave My back to those who struck Me, and my cheeks to those who plucked out the beard; I did not hide My face from shame and spitting" (Isaiah 50:6).

8. "His visage was marred more than any man, and His form more than the sons of men" (Isaiah 52:14).

9. "But He was wounded for our transgressions, He was bruised for our iniquities; the chastisement for our peace was upon Him, and by His stripes we are healed" (Isaiah 53:5).

10. "Now gather yourself in troops, O daughter of troops; he has laid siege against us; they will strike the judge of Israel with a rod on the cheek" (Micah 5:1).

11. "And I will pour on the house of David and on the inhabitants of Jerusalem the Spirit of grace and supplication; then they will look on Me whom they pierced. Yes, they will mourn for Him as one mourns for his only son, and grieve for Him as one grieves for a firstborn" (Zechariah 12:10).

12. "And one will say to him, 'What are these wounds between your arms?' Then he will answer, 'Those with which I was wounded in the house of my friends'" (Zechariah 13:6).

13. "Jesus answered and said to her, 'Whoever drinks of this water will thirst again, but whoever drinks of the water that I shall give him will never thirst. But the water that I shall give him will become in him a fountain of water springing up into everlasting life'" (John 4:13–14).

14. "On the last day, that great day of the feast, Jesus stood and cried out, saying, 'If anyone thirsts, let him come to Me and drink. He who believes in Me, as the Scripture has said, out of his heart will flow rivers of living water'" (John 7:37–38).

15. "And all drank the same spiritual drink. For they drank of that spiritual Rock that followed them, and that Rock was Christ" (1 Corinthians 10:4).

16. "Cursed is everyone who hangs on a tree" (Galatians 3:13).

17. "But God forbid that I should boast except in the cross of our Lord Jesus Christ, by whom the world has been crucified to me, and I to the world" (Galatians 6:14).

18. "And being found in appearance as a man, He humbled Himself and became obedient to the point of death, even the death of the cross" (Philippians 2:8).

19. "And according to the law almost all things are purified with blood, and without shedding of blood there is no remission" (Hebrews 9:22).

20. "Looking unto Jesus, the author and finisher of our faith, who for the joy that was set before Him endured the cross, despising the shame, and has sat down at the right hand of the throne of God" (Hebrews 12:2).

21. "Who Himself bore our sins in His own body on the tree, that we, having died to sins, might live for righteousness—by whose stripes you were healed" (1 Peter 2:24).

22. "Behold, He is coming with clouds, and every eye will see Him, even they who pierced Him. And all the tribes of the earth will mourn because of him. Even so, Amen" (Revelation 1:7).

23. "And He said to me, 'It is done! I am the Alpha and the Omega, the Beginning and the End. I will give of the fountain of the water of life freely to him who thirsts'" (Revelation 21:6).

LAST WORDS, FIRST STEPS

Chapter 5 Discussion Questions

1. Describe the last time you heard a detailed account of the passion of Christ's suffering.

2. Which aspect of Christ's physical suffering moves you the most?

3. What impact does reading about the intense suffering of Jesus have on you?

4. What if you were there when they crucified our Lord, what would your reaction be?

5. Why do you think Jesus had to suffer such a barbaric form of execution?

6. Is there any pain—physical or emotional—that the Lord Jesus hasn't experienced for us?

7. How can Jesus offer complete satisfaction for the deepest longings and thirsts of your soul?

It is finished.

—

John 19:30

CHAPTER 6

IT IS FINISHED

WORD OF PERFECTION

The casket is open with family and friends parading by. For many, painful images and missed opportunities flood their hearts in overwhelming grief:

"If only we had more time."

"If only we had done more together."

"If only we had fought less with each other."

But the deceased may have carried far greater burdens to the grave:

"I could've done so much more."

"I could've been there more for my family."

"If only I had finished that project, that promise."

"If only I could do it over . . ."

Shoulda! Coulda! Woulda! Sound familiar? Do you have unfinished business, unfinished achievements, unsatisfied debts and relationships? Where does it all end?

Our Constant Striving

Much of life revolves around working toward achievement, finishing a project, and realizing a goal. From the day you were born you were expected to finish things. First there was preschool, then elementary, then junior high, then high school, then college, then graduate school, then the bar exam, and so on. On top of all that came athletics, fine arts, merit badges, recitals, and scholastic achievements. We're a race of achievers, yet none of us has finished or accomplished *everything*—not on your life!

Not only are we bent on achievement, but we also judge others based on their achievements. We always have. We always will.

Perhaps the most devastating kind of striving involves our constant efforts to do "enough" good things to earn God's favor. We strive to pray enough, to read our Bibles enough, to minister enough, to do enough good works so that someday we will finally "finish." But this is a futile, exhausting, hopeless cycle—for in our own strength, we will never finish our spiritual journey.

How do we ever escape the crazy, endless, and insatiable cycle of finishing a task on our spiritual journey? How do we get to a point where we've done enough? What is enough? What does it mean to have finished something so that our future will be settled and satisfied for all eternity? Pressures from within and without drive us to finish, but truth be told—we don't. Failure, procrastination, and straight-out quitting mark all of us to some degree.

The One Who Finished

Then He came!—the One who would begin and finish things perfectly. He never quit, procrastinated, or cast blame.

> *I have* finished *the work which You have given Me to do.* (John 17:4)

He gave *one* sufficient answer, triumphantly proclaimed across the ages from the place called Calvary as the sixth recorded Word of Life spoken from the Tree of Death: "It is finished!"

Going all the way back to the beginning, the Bible teaches that God created the heavens and the earth in six days, and then He said it was "very good," and, in fact, "finished":

Thus the heavens and the earth, and all the host of them, were finished. (Genesis 2:1)

The work that atoned for sins and ushered in the reality of resurrection life was completed upon the Cross of suffering. It was so divinely perfect that God once again said, "It is finished."

Contrast that monumental task of eternal significance with our own human frailty to complete even the most menial of tasks.

The One charged with the most important job in the universe uttered the most life-giving words ever, words spoken from the most unseemly, humiliating, and cruelest spot on earth—a Roman cross.

The Babe of Bethlehem who was born in a livestock manger closed the deal—the largest and costliest transaction in all eternity.

The One who was despised, rejected, scourged, and pierced could say with authority from the lowliest of stations, "It is finished."

The only One who through His enduring obedience and selfless sacrifice could say from the loneliest of places, "It is finished"—giving sinners a clean bill of sale purchased by His own blood.

He breaks the power of cancelled sin,
He sets the prisoner free;
His blood can make the foulest clean,
His blood availed for me.[1]

What did Jesus mean when He said, "It is finished"? The phrase in Greek is one word, *tetelestai*, which comes from the root *teleo-,* meaning "to bring to an end, complete, fulfill."[2] This specific form of the verb appears only twice in the New Testament, both uttered by Jesus on the Cross: "After this, Jesus, knowing that *all things were now accomplished*, said that the Scripture might be fulfilled, 'I thirst.' . . . When Jesus had received the sour wine, He said, '*It is finished!*' And bowing His head, He gave up His spirit" (John 19:28, 30).

Hebrew scholar Dr. Michael Brown expounds on these words: "Although the verb *teleo* occurs twenty-eight times in the New Testament, the form *tetelestai* is found only twice, and those two occurrences are in the same context, right next to each other, making the meaning perfectly clear. Jesus was saying, 'Mission accomplished! Everything that had to be done has been done!'"[3]

At that moment in history, the divine mission was accomplished. Jesus had done it! Every sin was judged, and the total price of our redemption was paid in full. Brown observes, "That is the power of the blood of Jesus. That is the glory of the Son of God. That is the depth of the Father's love—and it was all for you and for me so that forever, we could be with Him and even share in His nature. Who could imagine such a story of love?"[4]

"It Is Finished"

We see the thread of God's perfect work woven through creation: *"it was very good"* (Genesis 1:31). We see it in redemption: *"it is finished."* And we see it in consummation of all things with the words—*it is done*—found at the end of the book of Revelation (21:6).

In creation what God made was "good." And He rested in celebratory triumph from His creative work. In redemption what Christ remade was good and He triumphantly declared, "It is finished," to rest from his tremendous labor.

Ultimately, we will see all things made new, and the new heaven and the new earth will be finished. The creation and the new creation are woven together in the tapestry of redemptive history in seamless profundity with one simple declaration: "It is finished!"

The Million-Dollar Question

What does the word *it* in "It is finished" precisely mean? Since the beginning of time man has been searching for *it*.

Remember the children's backyard game of tag? The player who is tagged searches for and chases down another to make the child "It" by touching him or her. But in the adult game of life, *it* is not something to be avoided—*it* is supposed to make me happy! When *it* is obtained, it means I've arrived. *It* may be that ever-elusive dream career, two-car garage, spouse and two kids, financial independence, and a comfortable retirement. *It* means true happiness.

But what does *it* look like? And how can I get some of *it* for myself?

The insatiable desire for *it* continues for millions of people traveling one hundred miles per hour down the "broad" way that "leads to destruction," looking and searching to find *it* (Matthew 7:13). Twice in the book of Proverbs Solomon tells us, "There is a way that seems right to a man, but its end [the pursuit of *it*] is the way of death" (Proverbs 14:12; 16:25).

Thankfully, there's an answer: the Calvary road, which leads lost sinners down the narrow way to Golgotha. There three crosses stand, and the Man in the Middle is Jesus Christ. This is where *it* is defined in, "*It* is finished." This is where one can say in true and eternal confidence: "I found *it*!"

Author John R. W. Stott explains that this "loud shout of victory" means "'it' has been and will forever remain 'finished.' We note the achievement Jesus claimed just before he died. It is not men who have finished their brutal deed; it is he who has accomplished what he came into the world to do."[5]

This profound statement of completion summarizes not only all other acts and statements of Christ, but also the other six Last Words from the Cross. Here's how:

"Father, Forgive Them for They Know Not What They Do"

The reservoir of forgiveness to unworthy sinners who know not what they do is once and for all secured, confirmed, and offered with the words, *"It is finished."*

"Today You Will Be with Me in Paradise"

Instant salvation, which was granted to the thief and all undeserving believers, is hereby sealed with the proclamation, *"It is finished."*

"Woman, Behold Thy Son!" "Disciple, Behold Thy Mother!"

Desperately needed grace for the neediest among us is now abundantly made available with His definitive words, *"It is finished."* Indeed, the very foundation of the church—the Body of Christ— rests firmly upon this mighty declaration.

"My God, My God,
Why Hast Thou Forsaken Me?"

The despised and forsaken One has emerged from the darkness, having conquered all the forces of hell and sin to victoriously declare, *"It is finished."*

"I Thirst"

His pain, suffering, and thirst are finally over, since, *"It is finished."*

"Father into Thy Hands
I Commend My Spirit"

The reality of ultimate peace and unbroken fellowship with the Father is restored and hastened by the words, "It is finished."

The Greatest Achievement

Repeatedly we find in the book of Hebrews the decisive phrase "once for all" (7:27; 9:12; 10:10). The writer of Hebrews can say this because Jesus' sacrifice was more powerful and effective than any that came before it. The imperfect Hebrew priests never sat down during their temple work because it was never finished. Hebrews 10:11 reads, "And every priest stands ministering daily and offering repeatedly the same sacrifices, which can never take away sins."

But Jesus, the perfect High Priest, offered one sacrifice that was complete, sufficient, and final. "But this Man, after He had offered one sacrifice for sins forever, sat down at the right hand of God" (Hebrews 10:12).

What rich language to describe what the *author* and *finisher* of our faith has "finished" and to demonstrate His superiority over all sacrifices and efforts ever performed.

The deal is sealed. Satan is defeated. Sin is conquered. The debt is paid. Salvation, healing, freedom, life, peace, joy, hope—all have been won. The shout of victory is proclaimed: It is done! It is completed! It is perfected! It is finished!

Here we see the infinite embodiment of achievement. No trophy case could contain the accolades due Jesus Christ (2 Timothy 2:2–8). No other king, president, religious leader, heavyweight champion, prophet, guru, moralist, scholar, celebrity, world leader, or any other human being has ever been able to declare, "It is finished."

Never before and never again will such a proclamation be heralded that will eternally save souls from hell and bring them abundant life right now.

> *My sin—O, the bliss of this glorious thought!—*
> *My sin—not in part but the whole,*
> *Is nailed to the cross and I bear it no more,*
> *Praise the Lord, praise the Lord, O my soul!*[6]

Is It Finished?

Is it finished? Look what happens when we slightly rearrange these profound words. The world has been asking this nagging question for millennia. *How much more religion do I need to get into heaven? How much more needs to be proven, accomplished, won, and earned? What more can I do to earn God's approval?*

As the world asks, "*Is* it finished?" Jesus boldly answers, "It is finished!" His finished work leads to our salvation and new beginning.

Tired of the Treadmill?

Even Christians tend to miss the significance of the word *tetelestai*. Like hamsters on a wheel we constantly clamor to gain the Father's acceptance. Even though He has finished the work, adopting us into His family—we're still trying to compete for a spot on God's roster!

So often believers tend to focus on what we do or have done for God. But these words of Christ shift our focus to what He has done for us. We simply get it backwards. As opposed to our efforts to finish and perform our way into God's favor, it is Christ's perfect effort that frees us to "walk in newness of life" (Romans 6:4).

I'll never forget the way a caller to my talk show once said it: "It's not about *performance-based acceptance*—me performing and God liking me and accepting me. It's about *acceptance-based performance*."

That is to say, Jesus Christ performed His perfect work and declared, "It is finished." God mercifully accepts me based on the achievement and perfection of His Son. My part is to respond like the second thief and to trust in His perfect work for my salvation.

It's also critical to remember that the gospel of Jesus Christ's finished work not only bought us salvation but also empowers our new life. The apostle Paul explains it this way: "He who has begun a good work in you will complete it until the day of Jesus Christ" (Philippians 1:6).

J. D. Greear explains, "The gospel not only tells us about the power of God; the message of the gospel is *itself* the power of God. . . . Believing the gospel is not only the way we become Christians, it is the power that enables us to do, every moment of every day, the very things Jesus commands us to do."[7]

The Grand Finale According to John

How providential that we find in John's Gospel this mighty declaration, "It is finished." John was the only disciple present to witness these words. Perhaps as he reflected on the words *It is finished,* his own Gospel flashed before his eyes:

- *The Living Word* gives us His final words (John 1:1).
- *The Water of Life* is poured out for the lost to find satisfaction (John 4:10).
- *The Bread of Life* is broken for the last time, enabling sinners to eat and be made righteous, never to hunger again (John 6:35).
- *The Light of the World* shines in a grand finale like none other (John 8:12).
- *The Good Shepherd* gives His life for His sheep once and for all (John 10:11).
- *The Resurrection and the Life* dies victoriously to be raised again (John 11:25).
- *The True Vine* bears His ultimate fruit (John 15:1).

The Lamb of God has been slain (John 1:29). The veil is torn (Matthew 27:51). New life is born and man has been set free. The work of creation was finished. The work of redemption is finished. All that's left is the ultimate new creation of heaven and earth—punctuated by the same words, "It is done" (Revelation 21:6).

He hung from the tree of death
So we could eat from the tree of life
The veil is torn; new fruit is born

His death has made man free
New life is here and hope is real
Because of that rugged tree.[8]

The notion that people can work their way into heaven by trying to be morally upright is absolutely repugnant to God because Jesus said, "It is finished!" How could we in our moral efforts and good deeds ever surpass the perfect, finished work of Christ on the Cross? Yet in the name of religion mankind tries to earn the favor of God that could only be earned by the finished work of Christ. Jesus paid it all!

Max Lucado says of this priceless declaration, "There are some facts that will never change. One fact is that you are forgiven. If you are in Christ, when he sees you, your sins are covered—he doesn't see them. He sees you better than you see yourself."[9]

"It is finished" is not only the divine punctuation mark on the six other words from the Cross, but it also covers the entire scope of all that Jesus Christ came to accomplish for all eternity.

Lifted up was he to die,
"It is finished!" was His cry;
now in heav'n exalted high:
Hallelujah, what a Savior.[10]

With these victorious words uttered from the Cross, Jesus Christ perfectly secured our peace with God. Next, we'll examine the seventh and final of these Last Words of Jesus as He rests in peace with God.

SCRIPTURAL REFLECTIONS
ON THE LAST WORDS OF JESUS

It Is Finished

1. "Thus the heavens and the earth, and all the host of them, were finished" (Genesis 2:1).

2. "Then I said, 'Behold, I come; in the scroll of the book it is written of me. I delight to do Your will, O my God, and Your law is within my heart'" (Psalm 40:7–8).

3. "This is the day the LORD has made; we will rejoice and be glad in it" (Psalm 118:24).

4. "He will swallow up death forever, and the Lord GOD will wipe away tears from all faces; the rebuke of His people He will take away from all the earth; for the LORD has spoken" (Isaiah 25:8).

5. "I, even I, am He who blots out your transgressions for My own sake; and I will not remember your sins" (Isaiah 43:25).

6. "For the Lord GOD will help me; therefore I will not be disgraced; therefore I have set My face like a flint, and I know that I will not be ashamed" (Isaiah 50:7).

7. "From that time Jesus began to show to His disciples that He must go to Jerusalem, and suffer many things from the elders and chief priests and scribes, and be killed, and be raised the third day" (Matthew 16:21).

8. "For even the Son of Man did not come to be served, but to serve, and to give His life a ransom for many" (Mark 10:45).

9. "For the Son of Man has come to seek and to save that which was lost" (Luke 19:10).

10. "So when Jesus had received the sour wine, He said, 'It is finished!' And bowing His head, He gave up His spirit" (John 19:30).

11. "For in him dwells all the fullness of the Godhead bodily; and you are complete in Him, who is the head of all principality and power" (Colossians 2:9–10).

12. "And you, being dead in your trespasses and the uncircumcision of your flesh, He has made alive together with Him, having forgiven you all trespasses, having wiped out the handwriting of requirements that was against us, which was contrary to us. And He has taken it out of the way, having nailed it to the cross" (Colossians 2:13–14).

13. "But when the kindness and the love of God our Savior toward man appeared, not by works of righteousness which we have done, but according to His mercy He saved us, through the washing of regeneration and renewing of the Holy Spirit" (Titus 3:4–5).

14. "Who being the brightness of His glory and the express image of His person, and upholding all things by the word of His power, when He had by Himself purged our sins, sat down on the right hand of the Majesty on high" (Hebrews 1:3).

15. "Inasmuch then as the children have partaken of flesh and blood, He Himself likewise shared in the same, that through death He might destroy him who had the power of death, that is, the devil" (Hebrews 2:14).

16. "By that will we have been sanctified through the offering of the body of Jesus Christ once for all. And every priest stands ministering daily and offering repeatedly the same sacrifices, which can never take away sins. But this Man, after He had offered one sacrifice for sins forever, sat down at the right hand of God, from that time waiting till His enemies are made His footstool. For by one offering He has perfected forever those who are being sanctified" (Hebrews 10:10–14).

LAST WORDS, FIRST STEPS

Chapter 6 Discussion Questions

1. Why are we so driven to achieve?

2. How have you ever failed or come short of accomplishing a goal?

3. How does Christ's perfection stand in stark contrast with the reality of our imperfection?

4. What does it mean for someone to be complete and fulfilled in Christ?

5. Is it possible to earn or achieve our way into God's perfect approval and salvation?

6. Why do we tend to get trapped on the endless performance treadmill of earning God's approval?

7. How can you truly experience Christ's finished work in your life?

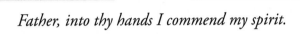

Father, into thy hands I commend my spirit.

—

Luke 23:46 KJV

FATHER, INTO THY HANDS I COMMEND MY SPIRIT

WORD OF PEACE

R.I.P. "Rest In Peace." You see it on tombstones; you hear it softly whispered at funerals. But what does this soulful balm exactly mean? While this is perhaps the most common phrase used by the living to commemorate the dead, how many people actually rest or die in peace? In Christ's final Word of Life from the Tree of Death we have the ultimate expression of resting in peace.

At 8:45 a.m. on September 11, 2001, the workday was just beginning at the Twin Towers of the World Trade Center in lower Manhattan. The 110-story steel and glass buildings were filled with as many as seventeen thousand people.

LAST WORDS OF JESUS

Thousands of secretaries, clerks, and executives were ascending and descending elevators, walking down hallways, settling into their desks, and talking with spouses to find out if the kids got to school on time. Others were chatting with coworkers about the Mets and Yankees at the coffee machines. On this late summer day, the early morning views from the upper floors of the Twin Towers were spectacular. With bright blue skies punctuated with puffs of billowy white clouds, it seemed one could see forever.

But in a tragic instant, all hell broke loose. That's when commercial jetliner Boston Flight 11, bound for Los Angeles before being hijacked and diverted, slammed into the North Tower with eighty-five passengers onboard at 8:46 a.m. Like a guided missile full of jet fuel traveling at 466 mph, it hit its target at the ninetieth floor. At 9:03 a.m. a second jetliner, also heavy-laden with fuel and bound for Los Angeles from Boston, torpedoed into the South Tower at 590 mph. Turned into towering pillars of fire, they imploded into thin air, creating a mushroom cloud of white ash. When the dust settled, nearly three thousand lives were lost on that terrible day. Many of these unfortunate souls succumbed to fiery heat and suffocating smoke. Others chose a different fate. Between 100 and 250 souls, trapped between the fire below and the locked doors at the top of the towers leading to the rooftop, leaped out of broken windows, choosing crushing impact to unspeakable incineration.

Whether on board the planes or inside the towers, no one knew what awaited them when they woke up that fateful morning.

The Real R.I.P.

Whether they live or die, Christians *rest* in peace by trusting Jesus for salvation. The consequences of not trusting Him are eternally devastating. Jesus warned that "broad is the way that leads to destruction" and "many" end up there (Matthew 7:13). Tragically, there's *no* "rest in peace" or peace in death for those who are spiritually lost because they refuse to accept the fruit of Christ's dying labor. The prophet Isaiah summed it up best:

> *"There is no peace," says the* LORD, *"for the wicked."*
> (Isaiah 48:22)

There is no peace, forgiveness, or pardon of sin by Christ for the "many" on the broad way to destruction. Those who have rejected His perfect, finished work choose instead to work their way right into hell (Ephesians 2:8–9). In this final Word of Life spoken from the Tree of Death, the Prince of Peace proclaims the greatest "Rest in Peace" statement in history.

Time and history are split by the Cross. A wooden Cross displays the only One able to act as *both* high priest and sacrificial lamb. He shines here on the Tree of Death as Mediator, Shepherd, Priest, Lamb, Intercessor, Messiah, King, Lord, Servant, Creator, Redeemer, Healer, Savior, Conqueror, and Deliverer. Still there was no "deceit in his mouth"—only His final Last Word: "Father, into thy hands I commend my spirit" (Luke 23:46 KJV).

Where do we first see the seventh cry from the Cross in Scripture? One thousand years earlier King David prayed, "Into Your hand I commit my spirit" (Psalm 31:5).

John MacArthur observes:

Psalm 31 is about the prayer of a righteous sufferer. The evening prayer of many of the Jews, their night prayer before going to bed like "Now I lay me down to sleep, I pray the Lord my soul to keep," but he added "Father": sweet communion is restored, punishment is over. And he omitted "thou has redeemed me, O Lord of truth" because he was the redeemer, not the one being redeemed.[1]

Paradise *lost* becomes paradise *gained* as this final Word of Life is heralded from the Tree of Death.

The Lord of the Sabbath rests from His work with a personal appeal to His . . .

"Father"

Twice in the seven recorded Last Words spoken from the Cross, Jesus addresses God as "Father"—first in the opening word of prayer, and here in these closing words. Much has transpired between "Father, forgive them" and "Father, into thy hands." Heaven and hell have collided in epic turmoil.

As we ponder this final Word of Life spoken from the Tree of Death, let us not miss the significance of the word *Father*. In his first formal sermon, the Sermon on the Mount, Jesus called God "Father" seventeen times. Then, in His final discussion with the disciples, He called God "Father" six times. John M. Drescher observes, "It was Jesus who taught us to call upon God as father in prayer. The word 'father' encompasses His whole concept of God throughout His life. And He invites us to speak to God, the creator, the sustainer and savior, in terms of closest affection."[2]

F. W. Krummacher comments, "The first word from his lips on earth was his father's name, and it is also the last. All his thoughts and deeds, desires and efforts, ended toward his Father and the glorifying of his name. To accomplish his

Father's will was his meat and drink; the love of his Father his delight and bliss; and union with him the summit of all his hopes and desires."[3]

Such affection is further reflected in Christ's ultimate statement of dependence:

"Father . . .

"Into Thy Hands"

Jesus places Himself into the very hands of God. Consider some of the numerous references throughout Scripture to God's mighty hands:

- Hand of redemption (Deuteronomy 7:8)
- Hand of direction (Psalm 78:72)
- Hand of power (Psalm 95:4)
- Hand of victory (Psalm 98:1)
- Hand of feeding (Psalm 104:28)
- Hand of judgment (Psalm 111:7; Hebrews 10:31)
- Hand of creation (Psalm 119:73; Isaiah 45:11–12)
- Hand of deliverance (Psalm 136:12)
- Hand of leading (Psalm 139:10)
- Hand of righteousness (Isaiah 41:10)
- Hand of protection (John 10:28)
- Hand of comfort (1 Peter 5:6–7)

The Son of God's hands are nailed to the Tree of Death, and all the while He is yielding His life into His Father's hands. In this manner of death, the Lord Jesus ushers in a new creation by redeeming mankind. His hands and feet are eternally involved in the redemption story.

I once heard Dr. Adrian Rogers ask on the radio, "What is the only man-made thing in heaven?" The answer: "The scars in the hands and feet and side of Jesus."

What better way to die than in the perfect place of the hands of the Father?

History comes full circle as . . .

- The pre-incarnate Christ creates the world—by His own hand.
- The incarnate Christ is led—by His Father's hand.
- The dying Christ commends His spirit—into the Father's hands.
- The risen Christ ascends—welcomed by the Father's hands.
- The Son of God now reigns—seated at His Father's right hand.

In fact, those who have received salvation from His hand can have the great hope the hymnist speaks of:

And now for me He stands before the Father's throne,
He shows His wounded hands, and names me as His own.
for me He died, for me He lives,
and everlasting life and light He freely gives.[4]

Have you reached for His hand, offering you the amazing grace of salvation?

Martyrs' Last Words

The martyr Stephen prayed a similar prayer in Acts 7:59: "Lord Jesus, receive my spirit."

How appropriate that the church's first martyr died praying both the first and last prayer of the One he followed. Stephen's *love* for Jesus shone brightly to indicate *intimacy* with Jesus as he bore the *pain* of Jesus at his own execution.

Note the powerful parallels between Jesus and Stephen. Like his Lord, Stephen:

- Was wrongfully accused of blasphemy (Acts 6:11)
- Died a brutal barbaric death (Acts 7:58, 60)
- Was accosted by a mob stirred by the religious leaders (Acts 6:12, Acts 7:54, 57)
- Was falsely accused by contrived witnesses (Acts 6:13–14)

- Witnessed Christ standing at the right hand of God (Acts 7:55)
- Was the only person in the Scriptures to speak two of the Words Jesus spoke from the Cross (Acts 7:59–60)
- Spoke two of the three Words of Christ that were prayers (Acts 7:59–60)
- Prayed Christ's last Words of Life—first (Acts 7:59)
- Prayed Christ's first Words of Life—last (Acts 7:60)
- Cried with a loud voice at his death (Acts 7:60)

A pattern of martyrs throughout history faithfully spoke these words as well. John Drescher notes that martyrs such as Thomas Becket, John Huss, Polycarp, and John Knox reportedly each prayed these final words of Christ in their final moments of life.

Martin Luther said in his last dying moments, "Blessed are they who die not only for the Lord as martyrs; not only in the Lord, as believers, but likewise with the Lord, as breathing forth their lives in the words, 'Father, into thy hands I commend my spirit.'"[5]

And it's with the strongest level of trust that He places Himself into God's all-powerful hands as demonstrated by the words . . .

"I Commend My Spirit"

Jesus is dying as He lived, commending and depending upon His Father. The One who brings us to God triumphantly commits Himself to God first. The six prior Last Words all lead to the seventh climactic Word.

Jesus rests in peace and paradise from His arduous labor because:

- Forgiveness upon the undeserving has been prayed.
- Pardon for the most unlikely has been imparted.
- Paternal care has been dispensed and the Body of Christ deployed.
- The Lamb has been forsaken to satisfy fully the Father's justice and wrath.
- His passion of thirst and suffering has reached its final point.
- The perfection of victory has been declared.

All that's left is for the Good Shepherd to utter this final Word and willingly give His life for the sheep (John 10:11, 17–18). A life not taken by the malicious minions of Satan, but rather laid down sacrificially at the appointed time.

It's no wonder so many faithful saints have died with this phrase on their lips. As you ponder this final Word of Life, ask yourself:

- What will be your last words?
- Will you die in peace?
- Does His peace keep your heart and mind?
  (Philippians 4:7)

All of this certainly gives us a fresh perspective on Solomon's words: "Death and life are in the power of the tongue" (Proverbs 18:21).

The One who spoke from the Cross had spoken across the darkness and created the world (Colossians 1:16). His word holds the world together (Hebrews 1:3). Jesus is "the Word" who is the very revelation of God to man (John 1:1).

His Final Breath

Observe how the Four Evangelists describe Jesus' final Word of Life from the Tree of Death:

- "And Jesus cried out again with a loud voice, and yielded up His spirit" (Matthew 27:50).
- "And Jesus cried out with a loud voice, and breathed His last" (Mark 15:37).
- "When Jesus had cried with a loud voice, He said, 'Father, "into Your hands I commit my spirit."' Having said this, He breathed His last" (Luke 23:46).

- "And bowing His head, He gave up His spirit" (John 19:30).

"He breathed His last" is a common ancient euphemism describing the moment of one's passing. But we know this was not Jesus' last breath, because He breathes out the Holy Spirit on His disciples after His resurrection:

And when He had said this, He breathed on them, and said to them, "Receive the Holy Spirit." (John 20:22)

Then some forty days later, the Holy Spirit is poured out again.

This time the whole world shakes—filling the Upper Room, where the disciples were gathered, with a mighty wind and tongues of flame, just as John the Baptist prophesied:

I indeed baptized you with water, but He will baptize you with the Holy Spirit. (Mark 1:8)

Thus, Jesus' final *breath* of rest expressed from the Cross set the stage for another momentous *breath* that changed the world after His resurrection.

That power was the Holy Spirit at Pentecost, setting into motion the fulfillment of John 14:12:

> He who believes in me, the works that I do he will do also; and greater works than these he will do, because I go to my Father.

Jesus Is Our Peace

Take a moment to meditate on Paul's eloquent summary of the peace wrought by Christ on the Cross:

> But now in Christ Jesus you who once were far off have been brought near by the blood of Christ. For He Himself is our peace, who has made both one, and has broken down the middle wall of separation, having abolished in His flesh the enmity, that is, the law of commandments contained in ordinances, so as to create in Himself one new man from the two, thus making peace, and that He might reconcile them both to God in one body through the cross, thereby putting to death the enmity. And He came and preached peace to you who were afar off and to those who were near. For through Him we both

have access by one Spirit to the Father. (Ephesians 2:13–18)

The war is over. Jesus' blood has been spilled. The savagery of the crucifixion is ended, and the humiliation and torture all lead to one reality—His glorious resurrection! He died and rose from the dead to bring life and peace.

- Is He your peace?
- Does the peace of God rule in your heart? (Colossians 3:15)
- Today, will you stop fighting the war and let His perfect peace conquer your soul?

Consider how peace was made with the Last Words of Jesus:

- His Word of Prayer: Forgiveness brings peace (Romans 5:1)
- His Word of Pardon: Instant peace granted to a life marked by conflict (Luke 23:43)
- His Word of Paternity: Peace to the widow, binding together the body of Christ (Ephesians 4:3, 15–16)
- His Word of Pain: The chastisement of our peace was upon Him (Isaiah 53:5)

- His Word of Passion: Peace to all who know the fellowship of His suffering (Philippians 3:10)
- His Word of Perfection: The ultimate peace plan— signed, sealed, and delivered! (Colossians 2:14–15)
- His Word of Peace: Resting in the peace of His Father's hands, while setting us at peace with God (Colossians 1:20)

Peace was proclaimed at Jesus' birth (Luke 2:14). Peace was publicly pronounced by His own parched lips at His death (Luke 23:46). Peace was poured out on the disciples after His resurrection (Luke 24:36; John 20:21).

Now you and I are invited to experience "the peace of God, which surpasses all understanding" (Philippians 4:7). But we'll never encounter the amazing peace of God until we first encounter the amazing God of peace. As one of my favorite bumper stickers simply states: "No Jesus, no peace. Know Jesus, know peace."

What Will You Do with Jesus Christ?

You've seen Him in His darkest moment, you've witnessed Him suffer like no other human, and you've heard Him speak. As you ponder these seven Words of Life from the Tree of Death, the question of the ages is now before you:

What will you do with Jesus Christ?

If you are not living in peace, you most certainly will not someday "rest in peace." Don't put it off—make peace with God today! Will you call out to Him like the lowly thief?

> You see, that is you and me on the cross. Naked, desolate, hopeless, and estranged. That is us. That is us asking . . .
>
> We don't boast. We don't produce our list. Any sacrifice appears silly when placed before God on a Cross. . . .
>
> We, like the thief, have one more prayer. And we, like the thief, pray.
>
> And we like the thief; hear the voice of grace.[6]

As you hear the Last Words of Jesus, what will your response be? Will you follow the crowd—or will you trust the One who laid down His life to give you life? Will you settle for a life of irrelevance or one of abundant meaning?

> The one who was wounded prayed, "Father forgive"
> The one who was robbed gave pardon to the thief
> He cared for the widow with a son and a place to live
> He was forsaken so we could be with Him

The Water of Life cried, "I thirst"
He said, "It is finished" for all to hear it
Then he cried, "Into thy hands I commend my spirit." [7]

I humbly invite you to respond with a heart like that of Peter, who, when asked by Jesus if he would also join the crowd of deserters, declared:

Lord, to whom shall we go? You have the words of eternal life. (John 6:68)

SCRIPTURAL REFLECTIONS
ON THE LAST WORDS OF JESUS

Father, into Thy Hands I Commend My Spirit

1. "Then God saw everything that He had made, and indeed it was very good. So the evening and the morning were the sixth day" (Genesis 1:31).

2. "And on the seventh day God ended His work which He had done, and He rested on the seventh day from all His work which He had done" (Genesis 2:2).

3. "In You, O Lord, I put my trust; let me never be ashamed; deliver me in Your righteousness" (Psalm 31:1).

4. "Into Your hand I commit my spirit; You have redeemed me, O Lord God of truth" (Psalm 31:5).

5. "But the meek shall inherit the earth; and shall delight themselves in the abundance of peace" (Psalm 37:11).

6. "Behold, the Lord God shall come with a strong hand, and His arm shall rule for Him; behold, His reward is with Him, and His work before Him" (Isaiah 40:10).

7. "Therefore My Father loves Me, because I lay down my life that I may take it again. No one takes it from Me,

but I lay it down of Myself. I have power to lay it down, and I have power to take it again. This command I have received from My Father" (John 10:17–18).

8. "And they stoned Stephen as he was calling on God and saying, 'Lord Jesus, receive my spirit'" (Acts 7:59).

9. "Therefore God also has highly exalted Him and given Him the name which is above every name, that at the name of Jesus every knee should bow, of those in heaven, and of those on earth, and of those under the earth, and that every tongue should confess that Jesus Christ is Lord, to the glory of God the Father" (Philippians 2:9–11).

1. "Now may the Lord of peace Himself give you peace always in every way. The Lord be with you all" (2 Thessalonians 3:16).

2. "There remains therefore a rest for the people of God. For he who has entered His rest has himself also ceased from his works, as God did from his" (Hebrews 4:9–10).

3. "And I heard a loud voice from heaven saying, 'Behold, the tabernacle of God is with men, and He will dwell with them, and they shall be His people. God Himself will be with them and be their God'" (Revelation 21:3).

LAST WORDS, FIRST STEPS

Chapter 7 Discussion Questions

1. Can people "rest in peace" in death if they've never experienced true peace in life?

2. Why is it significant that these are Jesus' *last* words but not His *final* words?

3. How trustworthy are the hands of God?

4. How would the people closest to you characterize your life: a life marked by His peace or by conflict?

5. What is the single greatest thing that is keeping you from receiving Jesus' perfect offer of salvation and peace right now?

6. How does the resurrection of Jesus relate to these Last Words of Jesus?

7. What will your response be to the dying words of Jesus Christ and the reality of resurrection?

ACKNOWLEDGMENTS

So many have graciously interacted with me on this journey. Even though I can't name you all, I thank you enthusiastically for all your wonderful feedback, prayers, and support.

It's an honor to dedicate this book to my wife, Jules, and our daughters, Hope, Gracie, Joy, and Faith. You deserve the highest accolades for traveling this long road with me. I'm especially grateful to Mom and Dad—"Big Stu" and Nancy Epperson—for believing in me and giving me the framework of faith that influenced everything I've written.

A huge thank you to the Worthy Inspired team—Byron, Jeana, Dennis, Alyson, Morgan, Pamela, and Jennifer—for your confidence in me and support throughout this process. Thanks for believing in me from day one! Ted Squires, I'm grateful for your immense wisdom and guidance throughout this process. Dr. Aaron Tabor, thanks for being an "iron sharpens iron" friend to me.

Thank you to Johnny Angel and Team Truth (our Truth Network family), for your amazing support. Chapter 3 is a tribute to the Boss Lady and all the "Moms of the Light" who heard this material first. You represent faithful mothers who deserve highest praise! And thank you Christian Car Guy, Robby Dilmore, for providing a Christlike example of social justice on the radio and in your godly testimony. Gregory Pittman Sr. and Jr.—I'm so grateful to both of you for blessing me with your story and letting me share it with the world.

I'd like to recognize Richie Kingsmore, Charles Billingsly, David and Apryl Roland, Phil Calhoun, and Frank Thomas for your tremendous help with the music portion of this project. Ralf Walters, Tim Muse, Dr. Ray St. John (Uncle Ray), Alex McFarland, and J. D. Greear—I truly appreciate your roles as editors, friends, researchers, theological sounding boards, and supporters, especially in the formative stages of this work.

In the early spring of 2012 the Lord burned this material on my heart as I was preparing for my weekly men's Bible study, Wednesdays in the Word. This is where this book was born, taught, and lived in real life with real men. Kerry, Phil, Jeff, Rusty, Hank, Wes, Larry, Bowersox, Ken, Sanger, Todd, Doug, Dale, Jon, Graham, Colin, Ron, Jumper, Jerry, Mark, Michael, Sam, Tony, Chuck, Randy, and Chetwood—love you guys and pray you will continue to hear His voice daily!

Additionally, I'm grateful to my NRB family and all those who broadcast the gospel of Jesus Christ across the airwaves. Dwight Gullion, you are to be praised for tirelessly helping me find many works on the Last Words of Jesus. I've been richly blessed by your friendship as well as your ministry. You represent Christian bookstores everywhere who faithfully steward the sacred trust of distributing Bibles and Christian literature.

I'm grateful to Jay, Chris, Khalim, and all my NCS "Iron Buddies" of the lodge, as well as many mentors and Christian friends who have built me up in the faith. Thank you to Pastor Rob Peters, Dr. Chapman, and all the wonderful people of Calvary Baptist Church and Day School—you have truly been a family to my family. Thanks for enduring all my sermons, devotions, and exhortations on the Last Words of Jesus.

My fondest regards go out to Dr. Erwin Lutzer. His book *Cries from the Cross* inspired me greatly on this pilgrimage. Early on, I approached him for his support, hoping the notion of my book on the same subject would not offend him. I'll never forget his response: "Young Stu, you can never write enough about the Cross of Christ." What an honor to learn from him, The Master's College faculty and staff, and so many other giants of the faith—both living and now in heaven. You'll see many of them listed in the "For

Further Study" section—that's an acknowledgments page as well.

Finally, a special thanks to you, the reader. As you've discovered, Jesus' eternal words are like no other. They won't appear on His tombstone because Jesus' last words were not His final words. The stone was rolled away! He's a living Savior whose Word is living, powerful, and sharper than any two-edged sword (Hebrews 4:12). I pray this book will lead you to take up His book, the Bible, and that you'll hear Him speak and be changed forever.

NOTES

Introduction: Words of Life from the Tree of Death
1. Stuart Epperson Jr., "Seven Words of Life from the Tree of Life," 2013.
2. Robert Jamieson, A. R. Fausset, and David Brown, *Fausset-Brown Bible Commentary,* vol. 3, *Matthew–Revelation* (Peabody, MA: Hendrickson, 1997), 475.
3. William Alexander, *Verbum Crucis* (London: Sampson Low, Marston, 1896), 108.

Chapter 1: Father, Forgive Them; for They Know Not What They Do
1. Lehman Strauss, *Listen! Our Dying Saviour Speaks* (Neptune, NJ: Loizeaux Brothers, 1987), 44.
2. Arthur W. Pink, *The Seven Sayings of the Saviour on the Cross* (Grand Rapids: Baker, 2005), 20.
3. Stuart Epperson Jr., "Seven Words of Life from the Tree of Death," 2013.
4. F. W. Krummacher, *The Suffering Saviour* (Grand Rapids: Baker, 1977), 382.
5. A. W. Tozer, *Who Put Jesus on the Cross?* (Harrisburg, PA: Christian Publications, 1975), 10.
6. Horatius Bonar, "I See the Crowd in Pilate's Hall," 1856.
7. Charles H. Spurgeon, *The Passion and Death of Christ* (Grand Rapids: Eerdmans, n.d.), 49.
8. *As We Forgive,* directed by Laura Waters Hinson (Owensboro, KY: Team Marketing, 2009), DVD.

9. Stephen E. Saint, "The Unfinished Mission to the 'Aucas,'" *Christianity Today*, March 1998, http://www.christianitytoday.com/ct/1998/march2/8t3042.html.

10. Michael Barry, *The Forgiveness Project: The Startling Discovery of How to Overcome Cancer, Find Health, and Achieve Peace* (Grand Rapids: Kregel, 2010), 88.

11. Mayo Clinic Staff, "Forgiveness: Letting Go of Grudges and Bitterness," November 11, 2014, http://www.mayoclinic.com/health/forgiveness/MH00131.

12. C. H. Spurgeon, "No. 166: Father, Forgive Them," Sermon Notes from Charles Spurgeon, http://www.gospelweb.net/SpurgeonSermonNotes/SpurgeonNotes166.htm.

Chapter 2: Today Shalt Thou Be with Me in Paradise

1. Warren W. Wiersbe, *The Bible Exposition Commentary*, vol. 5 (Colorado Springs: David C. Cook, 1992), 275.

2. Matthew Henry, *Matthew Henry Commentary*, vol. 1 (Grand Rapids: Zondervan, 1961), 1498.

3. Steven Furtick, *Seven-Mile Miracle: Experience the Last Words of Christ as Never Before* (Portland: Multnomah, 2013), DVD.

4. Strauss, *Listen!*, 44.

5. Stuart Epperson Jr., "Which Man Are You?," 2013.

6. Pink, *Seven Sayings*, 43.

7. Greg Laurie, "Sermons on Christ's Final Words," A New Beginning broadcast, spring 2011.

8. William Cowper, "There Is a Fountain Filled with Blood," 1772.

9. David Jeremiah, *Discover Paradise* (Nashville: Thomas Nelson, 2009), 89–90.

10. Strauss, *Listen!*, 33.

11. C. H. Spurgeon, *Christ's Words from the Cross* (Grand Rapids: Zondervan, 1993), 33.

Chapter 3: Woman, Behold Thy Son! . . . Disciple, Behold Thy Mother!

1. Jennifer L. Bach, "Acts of Remembrance: Mary Todd Lincoln and Her Husband's Memory," *Journal of the Abraham Lincoln Association*, 25 (Summer 2004): 25–49, http://hdl.handle.net/2027/spo.2629860.0025.204.
2. "Facts and Statistics," Orphan Hope International, http://www.orphanhopeintl.org/facts-statistics/.
3. R. C. Sproul, *John*, St. Andrew's Expositional Commentary (Lake Mary, FL; Reformation Trust Publishing, 2009), 368.
4. Josef Mohr, "Silent Night! Holy Night!" trans. John F. Young, 1863.
5. William C. Dix, "What Child Is This?," 1865.
6. John Calvin, *A Harmony of the Gospels Matthew, Mark and Luke; and James and Jude,* Calvin's New Testament Commentaries Series, vol. 3 (Grand Rapids: Eerdmans, 2000), 232.
7. Shane Claiborne, Jonathan Wilson-Hartgrove, Enuma Okoro, *"Holy Week: Palm Sunday,"* in *Common Prayer: A Liturgy for Ordinary Radicals* (Grand Rapids: Zondervan, 2010), 208.
8. Pink, *Seven Sayings*, 16.
9. Stephanie Samuel, "Churches' Dilemma: 80 Percent of Flock Is Inactive," *The Christian Post*, June 26, 2011, http://www.christianpost.com/news/authors-pastors-must-go-after-lost-sheep-to-increase-church-participation-51581/
10. Rob Peters, *Evangel-lies* (Xulon Press, 2007), 62.
11. K. S. Howard, J. E. B. Lefever, J. G. Borkowski, and T. L. Whitman, "Fathers' influence in the lives of children with adolescent mothers," *Journal of Family Psychology* 20, no. 3 (2006): 468–76.
12. Doris J. James, "Profile of Jail Inmates, 2002," Bureau of Justice Statistics Special Report, July 2004, http://www.bjs.gov/content/pub/pdf/pji02.pdf.
13. Center for Disease Control, quoted in Fatherhood/Factor, "U.S. Fatherhood Statistics," http://fatherhoodfactor.com/us-fatherless-statistics/.

14. Carrie Brown McWhorter, "Churches Seek to Meet State's Foster Care Needs," *The Alabama Baptist*, November 19, 2009, http://www.thealabamabaptist.org/print-edition-article-detail.php?id_art=13429&pricat_art=2.

15. The Turn-Around Agenda, "How It All Began," http://www.turnaroundagenda.org/howitbegan.

16. Robby Dilmore, personal conversation with the author, March 13, 2013.

Chapter 4: My God, My God, Why Hast Thou Forsaken Me?

1. Joel Beeke, "Christ Forsaken," *Tabletalk,* December 1, 2008, http://www.ligonier.org/learn/articles/christ-forsaken/.

2. Issac Watts, "At the Cross," in *Hymns and Spiritual Songs, in Three Books* Book 2, no. 9 (Wilmington, DE: Brynberg and Andrews, 1793).

3. John R. W. Stott, *The Cross of Christ* (Downers Grove, IL: InterVarsity, 1986), 329.

4. Krummacher, *Suffering Savior*, 413.

5. Alan D. Wright, *Free Yourself, Be Yourself: Find the Power to Escape Your Past* (Colorado Springs: Multnomah, 2010), 74.

6. Erwin W. Lutzer, *Cries from the Cross: A Journey into the Heart of Jesus* (Chicago: Moody, 2002), 98.

7. Watts, "At the Cross."

8. Timothy Keller, *King's Cross* (New York: Penguin Group, 2011), 201–2.

9. Alexander, *Verbum Crucis*, 109.

Chapter 5: I Thirst

1. African American spiritual, "Were You There When They Crucified My Lord?" first published in *William Barton's Old Plantation Hymns*, 1899.

2. Wright, *Free Yourself*, 72–73.

3. "Progress on Drinking Water and Sanitation: Special Focus on Sanitation," World Health Organization and United Nations Children's Fund Joint Monitoring Programme for Water

Supply and Sanitation, 2008, http://www.who.int/water_sanitation_health/monitoring/jmp_report_7_10_lores.pdf.

4. "100 Wells Campaign: Help Give a Community Water for Life," Persecution Project Foundation, http://www.100wellscampaign.com, accessed October 4, 2013.

5. Hank Hanegraaff, *Resurrection* (Nashville: Thomas Nelson, 2000), 19.

6. Cicero, *The Orations of Marcus Tullius Cicero*, vol. 4 (eBook #11080, Gutenberg.org, 2004), as quoted in "The Physical Death of Jesus," http://www.frugalsites.net/jesus/crucifixion.htm, accessed October 31, 2013.

7. Sproul, *John*, 357.

8. "O Sacred Head, Now Wounded," Latin poem, trans. and music James Waddel Alexander.

9. Lee Strobel, *The Case for Christ: A Journalist's Personal Investigation of the Evidence for Jesus* (Grand Rapids: Zondervan, 1998), 195.

10. Laurie, "Christ's Final Words."

11. Strobel, *Case for Christ*, 196.

12. Max Lucado, *He Chose the Nails* (Nashville: Thomas Nelson, 2000), 91–93.

13. Strobel, *Case for Christ*, 197–98.

14. Ibid.

15. Hanegraaff, *Resurrection*, 19.

16. Charles Wesley, "And Can It Be That I Should Gain?," 1738.

17. Wright, *Free Yourself*, 73–74.

18. Arthur Bennett, ed., *The Valley of Vision: A Collection of Puritan Prayers and Devotions* (Carlisle, PA: Banner of Truth Trust, 1975), 74.

19. Isaac Watts, "When I Survey the Wondrous Cross," 1707.

Chapter 6: It Is Finished

1. Charles Wesley, "Oh, for a Thousand Tongues to Sing," 1739.

2. "5055. teleó," Strong's Concordance, s.v. "teleó," Bible Hub, http://biblehub.com/greek/5055.htm.

3. Michael L. Brown, *Hyper-Grace: Exposing the Dangers of the Modern Grace Message* (Lake Mary, FL: Charisma House, 2014), 243–44.

4. Ibid.

5. Stott, *Cross of Christ*, 82.

6. Horatio G. Spafford, "It Is Well with My Soul," 1873.

7. J. D. Greear, *Gospel: Recovering the Power that Made Christianity* (Nashville: B&H, 2011), 103.

8. Stuart Epperson Jr., "Seven Words of Life from the Tree of Death," 2013.

9. Max Lucado, "April 4: The Debt Is Paid," in *Grace for the Moment: Inspirational Thoughts for Each Day of the Year* (Nashville: J. Countryman, 2000), 113.

10. Philip P. Bliss, "Hallelujah, What a Saviour!" 1875.

Chapter 7: Father, into Thy Hands I Commend My Spirit

1. John MacArthur, "The Crucifixion Chronicle" (sermon, Burbank, CA, October 2008), http://www.gty.org/products/Audio-Series/303/The-Crucifixion-Chronicle.

2. John M. Drescher, *Testimony of Triumph: The Meaning of Christ's Words from the Cross* (Grand Rapids: Zondervan, 1980), 89–90.

3. Krummacher, *Suffering Savior*, 438–39.

4. Norman J. Clayton, "My Hope Is in the Lord" (Los Angeles: Norman J. Clayton Publishing, 1945).

5. Drescher, *Testimony of Triumph*, 89.

6. Lucado, "April 28: Voice of Grace," in *Grace for the Moment*, 137.

7. Stuart Epperson Jr., "Seven Words of Life from the Tree of Death," 2013.

FOR FURTHER STUDY ON CHRIST'S LAST WORDS

A vast amount of material exists on the Last Words of Jesus. Following is a list of many—but certainly not all—works specifically dedicated to this subject. Additional resources can be found online at LastWordsofJesus.com.

Alexander, William. *Verbum Crucis.* London: Sampson Low, Marston, 1896.

Butler, John G. *Jesus Christ, His Crucifixion.* Clinton, IA: LBC, 2005.

Drescher, John M. *Testimony of Triumph: The Meaning of Christ's Words from the Cross.* Grand Rapids: Zondervan, 1980.

Evans, Craig A. and N. T. Wright. *Jesus: The Final Days.* Louisville: Westminster John Knox, 2009.

Ford, W. Herschel. *Seven Simple Sermons on the Savior's Last Words.* Grand Rapids: Zondervan, 1953.

Furtick, Stephen. *Seven Mile Miracle.* Portland: Multnomah, 2013. DVD.

Girod, Gordon H. *Words and Wonders of the Cross.* Grand Rapids: Baker, 1962.

Hamilton, Adam. *Final Words.* Nashville: Abingdon, 2011.

Hengel, Martin. *Crucifixion.* Philadelphia: Fortress, 1977.

Hunt, June. *Forgiveness.* Torrance, CA: Aspire, 2013.

Jones, Russell Bradley. *Gold from Golgotha.* Chicago: Moody, 1945.

Keller, Tim. *King's Cross.* New York: Penguin, 2011.

Kendall, R. T. *Total Forgiveness*. Lake Mary, FL: Charisma House, 2007.

Krummacher, F. W. *The Suffering Saviour*. Grand Rapids: Baker, 1977.

Hayford, Jack. *How to Live Through a Bad Day*. Nashville: Thomas Nelson, 2001.

Laurie, Greg. *Finding Hope in the Last Words of Jesus*. Grand Rapids: Baker, 2009.

Lockyer, Herbert. *All the Messianic Prophecies of the Bible*. Grand Rapids: Zondervan, 1973.

Lutzer, Erwin. *Cries from the Cross*. Chicago: Moody, 2002.

MacArthur, John F., Jr. *The Murder of Jesus*. Nashville: Word, 2000.

Pink, Arthur W. *The Seven Sayings of the Saviour on the Cross*. Grand Rapids: Baker, 2005.

Spurgeon, C. H. *Christ's Words from the Cross*. Grand Rapids: Zondervan, 1993.

Spurgeon, Charles H. *The Passion and Death of Christ*. Grand Rapids: Eerdmans, n.d.

Stott, John R. W. *The Cross of Christ*. Downers Grove, IL: Inter-Varsity, 1986.

Strauss, Lehman. *Listen! Our Dying Saviour Speaks*. Neptune, NJ: Loizeaux Brothers, 1965.

Strobel, Lee. *The Case for Christ*. Grand Rapids: Zondervan, 1998.

Tozer, A. W. *Who Put Jesus on the Cross?* Harrisburg, PA: Christian Publications, 1975.

Williams, Clayton. *The Dark Road to Triumph*. Binghamton, NY: Vail-Ballou, 1960.

Wilson, Ralph F. *Seven Last Words of Christ from the Cross*. Loomis, CA: Jesus Walk Publications, 2009.

Wisloff, Fredrik. *With Him to Golgotha*. New Ipswich, NH: Pietan, 2007.

Zugibe, Frederick T. *The Crucifixion of Jesus*. New York: M. Evans, 2005.

ABOUT THE AUTHOR

Stu Epperson Jr., BA, MS, is founder and president of The Truth Network, with radio stations across North Carolina, central Iowa, and Salt Lake City. Truth Network also develops and syndicates programs on over 300 affiliates nationwide. In his spare time Stu hosts *Truth Talk Live*, his own nationally syndicated show, and he coaches and mentors through the game of basketball. His passion is that all people everywhere will experience truth. Stu lives in Winston-Salem, North Carolina, with his wife, Julie, and their four daughters.

WORTHY
Inspired

If you enjoyed this book, will you consider sharing
the message with others?

- Mention the book in a Facebook post, Twitter update, Pinterest pin, blog post, or upload a picture through Instagram.
- Recommend this book to those in your small group, book club, workplace, and classes.
- Head over to facebook.com/worthypublishing, "LIKE" the page, and post a comment as to what you enjoyed the most.
- Tweet "I recommend reading #LastWordsofJesus by stuepperson//@worthypub"
- Pick up a copy for someone you know who would be challenged and encouraged by this message.
- Write a book review online.

You can subscribe to Worthy Publishing's
newsletter at worthypublishing.com.

Worthy Publishing Facebook Page   Worthy Publishing Website